WHEN IT RAINS, IT POURS

A Memoir

Elle Shane

Archway Publishing books may be ordered through booksellers or by contacting:

Archway Publishing
1663 Liberty Drive
Bloomington, IN 47403
www.archwaypublishing.com
844-669-3957

ISBN: 978-1-6657-0221-8 (sc)
ISBN: 978-1-6657-0222-5 (e)

Library of Congress Control Number: 2021901932

Print information available on the last page.

Archway Publishing rev. date: 02/16/2021

Thank you to my best friend. You've known me since second grade; even though it was a struggle, you didn't give up on me. You were there when I needed someone to talk to, and you reminded me that I wasn't crazy, even in my lowest times. After all those years, you're still right by my side. You saw everything that happened to me, and we made promises that you never broke. Thank you. I love you a lot!

I want to thank my soul mate; the most important person in my life. Thank you for believing in me and never giving up and always cheering me on. You have supported me, and you have stuck by my side, no matter how hard the times got. You never rushed me to feel better; you just patiently waited and loved me—even on my ugliest days. You never let me forget about my dreams, and you pushed me to keep going, even when I thought I couldn't do it. I really couldn't have gotten to where I am if not for you rooting me on. I love you!

When I was younger, I had no idea what was in store for me. As humans, we don't, right? I sure wish I had known, though. So many events, incident's, and experiences happen in one's life, and those aren't always sunshine and rainbows—at least I don't remember any sunshine and rainbows—but I learned to find the light in the darkest of places. Things happen, and people change. It isn't always easy, but we suck it up and manage. I don't know how others deal; I push it into spaces in the back of my mind and try to forget about it. It's almost like I have tiny storage boxes containing all those thoughts. The boxes finally have gotten so full that they're bursting out, and my mind is about to explode. That wouldn't be good for any of us, so I have written it all out.

**Everyone
has a story to tell.
Here's mine.**

CONTENTS

Chapter One 1

Chapter Two 22

Chapter Three 42

Chapter Four 64

Chapter Five 85

Chapter Six 98

Chapter Seven 104

Chapter Eight 126

Chapter Nine 135

Chapter Ten 144

Chapter Eleven 159

Chapter Twelve 182

Chapter Thirteen 190

—

broth·er

/ˈbrəT_Hər/

noun

a man or boy in relation to other sons and
daughters of his parents

When I was little, my mom and my sister both would
tell me, "He's not your brother," any time my sister
talked about him. He was her brother but not mine. I
felt like I wasn't really part of the family, and I didn't
fit into the puzzle. I've always had a feeling of emp-
tiness, but I have had memories of him, of us, ever
since I was little. I don't know where these memories
came from since they weren't necessarily real, but
it was always a good feeling to close my eyes and
see him, my sister, and me, playing together. They

seemed so real because I wished so hard to have actually lived them.

Jane was the only sibling I knew I had besides my half-sister, Hannah, from my mom; no one told me any differently. It was a month before my nineteenth birthday when the phone rang. My mom was in her room, doing God knows what, and it took her a bit longer than it should have to answer the phone. It probably didn't help that she had mounds of clothes and heaps of junk she had bought the Sunday before at the local thrift store—she went every Sunday for the twenty-five-cent sale. Even if she didn't need anything, she thought that somehow, she could turn it around and profit from it—even though most of it was useless, and she never did anything with any of it. She had to maneuver around it. My mom had too many clothes, and they filled the closet and half of the floor.

From one room over and down the hallway, I heard my mom say, "Jane, it's for you. It's Nick."

My sister's brother was calling, presumably to catch up and see how she was doing. I slid down the wall near the doorway between our rooms and pressed my ear to the wall. I got as close as possible, as if I were one with the wall. I closed my eyes and wished I was a fly on the other side, hovering just above the ceiling fan. I wanted so badly to hear what was said, and I pretended I was a part of their conversation. There was a lot of "oh yeah," and "cool," along with laughter coming from the other room. Only silence came from my end of the conversation. I closed my eyes again and wished that I had a brother like Nick to call me, but that's wishful thinking. Jane was my only sibling I had besides Hannah.

Suddenly, it got quiet on her end, and then I heard my mom talking, but she wasn't talking to Jane, so she must have been talking to Nick. I didn't understand why she needed to talk to him; he wasn't her biological son. I heard her mumble "mm-hm," and then I heard the shuffle of her small feet down the short hallway.

Within seconds, she knocked on my door and said, "Elle, the phone!" I could almost hear the annoyance from the huff of air she let out. As the door swung open, I jumped up on my bed. I didn't want her to ask me why I was awkwardly sitting on the floor by the door. I didn't want to answer that question with the truth. Again, she said, "Elle, for you. Here!" She almost shoved the phone in my face with even more annoyance.

My hand was a little shaky as I reached for the phone, and my heart was pounding from both fear and excitement. I thought, *Why does Nick want to talk to me, anyway? How does he know my name?* When my mom went to the other room, I could hear angry whispers coming from Jane. She too was annoyed and seemed envious that our mom had interrupted her conversation with Nick. She seemed extremely pissed off that my mom had cut their conversation short, but I guess I would have been too.

I closed my eyes as I put the phone to my ear, but I didn't say a word. I think he heard my confusion from the breath of air that escaped my mouth as I finally said, in a tiny voice, "Hello?"

"Hey. It's Nick," he said. His words lingered in the quiet room. The silence on my end was almost deafening; he had to be wondering if I was still there. He spoke quickly as if he was afraid I would hang up. "Your mom just told me I have another sister,"

"Yeah? Okay. . . .." I rolled my eyes because I didn't see why he wanted to tell me that.

"Yeah, it's you,"

A whirlwind of emotions went through me. There was sadness because for all these years, I'd had no idea he was my brother. There was anger because my mom had kept it from us, but I also felt anger toward him for never asking. Most of all, though, I was excited to try to know him. "Are you *sure,* sure? Like, positively sure?" I asked in almost a squeal.

"Of course, I'm sure!" He almost shouted it because he was so thrilled. He then explained that the three of us—he, Jane and I—had the same dad but different moms. He apologized for not finding out sooner and said he wished he could have been the big brother to me that he knew I'd needed, years earlier.

We talked for what seemed like hours, even though it was only about forty-five minutes. Those minutes brought me so much joy, and that was a feeling I had forgotten I could feel. We laughed, and he asked about me. I wasn't too familiar with being asked about myself, even by my family. They always shrugged me off, as if something was wrong with me. It felt so good that someone was interested in how I was doing.

Nick got on a plane from New Jersey to Oklahoma within a few days of our talking so we could finally meet. I made a big sign to hold so he'd be able to recognize me. It read, "Welcome, Nick!" My mom had me add at the bottom of the sign: "after 21 years." I assumed this was for extra attention from everyone else; that was something she just did for her pleasure. Jane was twenty-one years old, so my mom once again managed to make it all about Jane instead of me *too*.

My mom made me feel like it should have been Jane holding that sign instead of me holding it.

My stepdad Mark, Jane, my mom, and I were at the airport to greet Nick. I was so anxious, waiting for someone I didn't know. I wasn't even sure what he looked like. My mind said how dumb it was of me to make a sign, and I almost threw it away, but I thought about how many people probably did the same thing to welcome their family or friends.

I looked at Jane; she didn't look too excited to see her brother, whom she hadn't seen in so long, but I ignored it. The baby in her stomach was probably making her tired.

Loads of people came walking in from the gate entrance, and my eyes darted all around. I wasn't sure who I was looking for, but I didn't want to stop searching. Ten minutes passed by, and there were still tons of people filing through the terminal. There were lots of happy screams and people hugging each other. In that second, I let my emotions get the best of me, and I felt myself becoming sad. Being let down was a feeling that had become normal. I remember dropping my head as I lowered the sign to the ground, and I walked over to lean on the wall.

Time just kept ticking by. I felt the warmth of tears

forming behind my eyelids, and a part of my heart was tearing, but when I looked up, my emotions seemed to fade away. I targeted a guy who looked to be the same age as Nick, walking through security. Again, I didn't know what he looked like, but I just knew it was him. You know the feeling in your gut that you get about certain situations, like intuition? That was my exact feeling.

When his eyes met mine, I immediately started grinning. My body was consumed with so much excitement that it gave me chills. We started toward each other in what was like a slow sprint. Everything seemed to pause for this moment, and soon, we were the only people around. He dropped all his luggage to scoop me up in a big bear hug. Passersby in the airport had stopped to watch us, and everyone was smiling in awe. We swung around in circles, and I didn't want to let go.

Jane walked up, so Nick set my feet on the ground. Then he turned to her. It was an awkward moment for them. He was smiling ear to ear as he reached for a hug, but she didn't even uncross her arms as she leaned in. It was like he had to give her a "bro hug," as if she were his long-lost friend. She did a half-smile and then hurried back to my mom's side. I shed a few happy tears because I was finally meeting *my* brother. A piece of me I wasn't fully aware was missing had been returned.

Thanksgiving was in just two weeks, and I had so much to be thankful for, more than I had been thankful for in so long. My mom and Mark set up space at the house for Nick to stay. He planned to be there for a week, and my mom didn't want him to get a hotel room. After he settled in, we went for a walk so I could show him around my neighborhood. Luckily, he was packed for the cold since it was chilly in New Jersey too. The air was so cold that it cut right through like tiny needles. It felt as if God had left a giant freezer door open above us, and the sky looked like it was going to snow.

Nick and I had walked about half a mile when we stopped at a well-known fast-food place because he said he didn't know what it was. I couldn't believe it! This was one of my favorite places to eat at. I ordered us a large chili cheese tots and two slushes. I'm not sure why I ordered slushes in November, but they were delicious. We sat at a small table, and I scooted my chair closer to his. He popped a tater tot, covered in chili and cheese, into his mouth even though I could see it was steaming hot.

"Damn! You weren't joking," Nick said. "That's the best thing I've eaten in a while!"

We shoveled the food into our mouths while talking about anything and everything. We took so many pictures together, even blurry ones. I just wanted to document every moment.

The next day, my mom suggested we all to go to Kansas City, Missouri, to show Nick the cool places around there. He had a rental car and invited Jane and me to ride with him. I ran over to the passenger side, laughing and yelling "Shotgun!" When we were kids, Jane and I always had done that when we rode in the car. This time, though, she didn't seem to care as she opened the back door and slid in. Jane looked completely lost and kept asking me if mom's car was still in front of us. She even complained about the music being too loud. I wasn't aware that my sister had become an eighty-year-old.

At some point, it got too annoying for Nick, and, of course, I was annoyed too. He had me call my mom to tell them to pull over. Nick told Jane she should get in the car with Mark and our mom; she didn't seem to have a problem doing that. I was confused and felt embarrassed for her to be acting so childish. I don't understand why people get so embarrassed about other's behavior, but I always did when it came to my mom and Jane. Our brother was with us, for Christ's sake, yet here she was, up our mom's ass.

Not having Jane in the car wasn't much of a loss. We turned up the radio and jammed to the music. Just being in the car with Nick was so much fun. It didn't matter what we did, as long as I was with him. I belted out the lyrics as he strummed on the steering wheel like we were in a band. He was so good at drumming that I stopped singing to watch him; he told me he played the drums back home. *I have the coolest brother,* I thought.

We finally made it to Kansas City. It was the longest car ride ever, but I was glad I'd ridden with him. I could only imagine how *not* fun it was to be in the car with Jane and them. My mom flagged us down, and we pulled into the parking lot of one of those discount ticket/visitor centers to figure out what we wanted to do first. My mom hopped out of the car and bolted inside as fast as a rabbit running from a predator. We followed shortly after, but Mark stayed behind in the car. Nick and I were looking at fliers for different attractions. I looked at the front counter and saw my mom. I got a gut feeling that she was making up some bullshit story to the lady working, so I told my brother

I would be right back and walked up to the counter. Sadly, I was right.

My mom was using my and Nick's story of finally meeting after so long to try to get free tickets or bigger discounts for other things. She wanted to spend as little money as possible, and she would do anything she could to save a dime. I heard her tell the lady that she was in the middle of directing a film about the story of our finally meeting. She already had all the actors, and she just needed to have it filmed. What the actual fuck? The story she told wasn't completely true. I was annoyed and extremely embarrassed, but luckily, Nick picked up on that quickly, so he said that we should leave and go do something. Then we could meet up with them later. I agreed and told my mom. She seemed upset, but I didn't care. I had no reason to impress the woman at the ticket desk, and neither did she.

We went shopping and enjoyed spending time together. It was getting close to dinnertime, and we were starving, so I called my mom to tell her we were going to eat and wanted them to join us. I didn't necessarily want them to join us, but Nick wanted Jane to be there. I knew that the only way she would come was if my mom and Mark were there too.

Nick chose a seafood place because I'd told him earlier it was one of my favorite places in KC. It was pricey but to my surprise the cost didn't matter to him. When we all sat at our table, which was bigger than we needed for just five of us, my mom sat a couple of seats away. Mark did so also; I assumed that was so he didn't piss off my mom.

Nick told Jane and me to get whatever we wanted because he was paying. He spent well over one hundred dollars on our three entrees; something else I wasn't used to. If we ate out it was always from the dollar menu. My mom told Mark that they would get nachos and share them. She didn't fool me; I knew exactly what she was trying to do. She often used the broke pity card to try to get someone to pay for her, but it didn't work with my brother. I understood not wanting to spend a lot of money sometimes, but this was a special occasion yet that didn't seem to matter to her. I was getting tired of never having money to do nice things and being frowned upon anytime I had something nice.

The next day, when we were back in Oklahoma, we all decided to get a bite to eat. Nick hadn't had much time to talk to Jane, so he wanted to talk over lunch. We chose a fast-food place since we had plans for dinner later, and we didn't mention our dinner plans to Mark, my mom or Jane because of how the last dinner with them had gone. Jane and my mom sat across from Nick and me; Mark sat at a nearby table, which he did often. I always joked that he was embarrassed by us so that's why he never sat with us, but I believed there was a little bit of truth to that.

Our number got called, so Nick got up to get our food. My mom gave me her judgmental wide-eyed look as he walked to the counter. I just rolled my eyes. Rolling my eyes had become such a normal thing that sometimes I didn't realize I was doing it. Nick returned moments later.

When they called my mom and Jane's number, he offered to get it for them. My mom didn't say, "No, that's okay," or "Thanks," she just expected him to do it. She was the queen, and everyone else were her peasants. We had some small talk, but Jane didn't say much. At first, I thought it was because she was focusing on food since she was eating for two. Nick asked Jane how she felt about being pregnant and if she was ready.

She opened her mouth to speak, but my mom cut her off and told Nick it was none of his business. Their conversation was something like this:

"She is my sister, and I would like to talk to her. I wasn't speaking to you."

"The doctors drugged her, so she doesn't know how to talk for herself. That's why I'm her guardian ad litem."

"That's bullshit. If you would just let Jane speak. . ."

"You're just like your father," my mom said, cutting him off just as fast as she had done to Jane. "Ian always thought he knew best, as do you. Jane needs me, and I make the decisions for her since she can't make them herself."

"I'll be damn well surprised if that baby comes out without any problems. It's going to have one hell of a life with you around."

I was shocked, and I could tell Jane was too. I felt like a deer in headlights and had no clue what to say. Jane looked trapped, like she had so much to say but couldn't form the words. I could tell she was upset, but I couldn't figure out who had upset her.

Nick got up and said he was leaving; that he was going to get an extended-stay hotel. He asked me if I was coming. I was torn between which decision would be better. I didn't want my mom mad at me, but I also didn't want to leave Jane. Ultimately, I didn't want to miss out on spending time with my brother.

I looked at my mom, and I saw so much anger and hatred. There was so much that I could almost see the steam coming out of her ears. I told her she was in the wrong, spitting the words as I spoke, and then I stood up and left with Nick. My mom was mad at me often, so what difference would it make? I mouthed the words "I'm sorry" to Jane and gave a pleading look to Mark. He just shook his head, shrugged and dipped a few of fries in his ranch dressing.

When we got to the hotel, Nick told me that he hadn't been comfortable with staying at my house anyway because it was too messy and small. I didn't blame him; it bothered me too, yet I lived there. I had nowhere else to go at the time. I never invited people over because our house wasn't "nice," and there was so much clutter everywhere. We even had roaches that my mom's brother had brought with him from Illinois when he was homeless. I didn't want other people to see them running down the wall like I did every day. When my mom or Mark would smash one on the wall, it stayed there. Every day I would see the roach guts and be reminded of the mess I lived in. I covered my head with a pillow, blanket or my hair because I had a fear that a roach would crawl into my ear and leave eggs inside. I lucked out that no one had seen a roach crawl out of my binder as I took it from my backpack when I was in middle school. Thinking about it made my skin crawl.

Deep down, I had hoped Nick would get a hotel in the beginning anyway. Suddenly, he told me he would be leaving in three days. My heart instantly shattered. All I wanted to do was cover my face with a pillow and scream. I was so furious that my mom was ruining this for me. I had spent so much of my childhood letting my mom control everything. I thought it was okay then, but I realized that it wasn't okay. I asked Nick if I could stay with him for the rest of the time he was here, and, thankfully, he said yes. It was going to be like a mini-vacation, and I was excited that I didn't have to be around my mom. I could pretend to be somewhere other than the place I hated most.

When I told my mom that I was staying with him, she told me I was wrong for picking sides with some-one other than her—and with him, of all people. She explained that he was wrong about everything he said, and he was just like our dad. But how would I even know? I didn't know anything about our dad either. I often found myself pushing the "mute" button on my phone when I talked to her so I could bitch as she spoke. I got off the phone after a few minutes of her nagging me. Nick and I decided to go out and see what we could do that night.

When we returned to the hotel room, my mom called me again. I sighed because I had a bad feeling about how the call would go, so I got out of earshot of Nick. That made him turn the TV volume down and focus on my conversation. She was yelling at me, so even if he hadn't turned down the TV, I'm sure he would have heard her. She said that I had betrayed her. I closed my eyes and just tried to keep calm. My mom had said that more often than not over the last few years, and I was getting used to hearing it, so I let her continue.

Then she said something along the lines of, "You're only staying in that hotel room with your brother so you can sleep with him. I knew he would single you out and take advantage of you. I didn't think you would do that."

My jaw dropped. A breath of shock and horror slid out between my lips, and I felt my face heat up. So many things came to mind that I wanted to say, to scream at her, but all that I could say was, "Fuck off."

I shut my phone off and threw it on my bed. I threw it harder than I thought because it bounced from the pillow and hit the wall with a thud. That was the first time I'd ever had the strength to stand up to my mom. I couldn't wrap my brain around the shit she had said to me.

Nick stood up and walked over to my bed. I told him everything she had said, and he looked as though he could kill someone. I couldn't blame him. Why would anyone say that to her kid, let alone about a sibling?

The next morning, he called the airlines to make sure they had his ticket switched. My mom had ruined everything.

We spent as much time together in those last three days as humanly possible. I was in college, so he would drop me off at class and then go to the gym nearby until my class was over. I always thought it was funny how much he liked the gym and how much I didn't care for it, until then. (I've become a mini-Nick and practically live at the gym when I'm not working.) I occasionally wondered how much we had in common.

We spent every second of my free time together after class. Nick wanted to take me to dinner since he would be gone by my birthday. I invited a couple of my good friends to come with us. I chose a local burger joint, and I must say those were the best burgers I ever had. I'm sure it was because I was eating them with people who meant the most to me.

We were on our last few bites when I got a brilliant idea. I told Nick that we should get matching tattoos. His body was covered in tattoos, and I only had two. He laughed and asked if I was sure. I was, and he agreed. I rode with my friend and thought of different ideas of tattoos. I was stupidly giddy as I started naming off my ideas to my friend. It was almost eight o'clock when we got to the tattoo shop, but luckily, one girl was still there, and she said that since we were getting small tattoos, she would do it. I was thrilled! We ended up getting puzzle pieces that would form a heart when they were connected. After all, he was the missing piece to the puzzle, and he filled the small hole in my heart.

There were so many things I wanted us to do in the days before he went back to New Jersey, but we didn't have much time. I was so upset and annoyed that he wouldn't stay as long as he'd planned in the first place, but I wasn't upset with him; I couldn't be. I wouldn't want to stay in a place where someone pushed all the wrong buttons for me either, and that's exactly what my mom did to him. I asked Nick about Ian, our dad. I learned so much in so little time but not enough.

He didn't talk to our dad anymore because our dad and his mom had split up when he was a teenager. One of the stories Nick told me was that our dad and uncle beat the neighbor's dog until it almost stopped breathing, right in front of Nick, because it barked so much. "Gotta teach it a lesson," while he chuckled to his son. Nick was a small child then. He kept repeating how shitty our dad had treated him over the years and said I wasn't missing much.

Immediately, I thought, *"Great. My biological father is screwed up like my mom. Lucky me."* The last hours flew by, and before I knew it, it was time for Nick to catch his flight back home. I was super-bummed. We hugged for so long, and he promised me that he would call and keep in touch. As he walked towards the gate to board the plane, tears welled up in my eyes and slid down my cheeks just as quickly as they had formed. I didn't want to let go of his hand.

Once Nick was out of view, I still stood in the same spot hoping he would turn around and come back, but he never did. I learned so much from him about our dad, but there was still a void that needed to be filled, and even more, there were so many questions that had to be answered.

Nick,

I'm so proud of you. You never let our dad ruin your life. I'm envious of how strong you are emotionally, and I wish I could have been stronger when our dad reached out to me. I want to thank you for being there for me, though. Meeting you was one of the best days of my life, and I'm so thankful that it happened. I know we're both busy with our lives, but I will always make sure we stay in contact!

I love you so much!

Elle

CHAPTER TWO

bi·o·log·i·cal
/ˌbīəˈläjək(ə)l/

noun
relating to biology or living organisms

The perfect father is someone who loves unconditionally and cares for his children; someone who supports the choices and decisions his children make—a person who never gives up, no matter how hard things get. The perfect father is who I wish Ian had been to me.

Ian was only eighteen, and my mom was about thirty-four when they got married. I didn't know much about him except that he was discharged from the military for his mental well-being because he was so-called crazy. At least that's what my mom had always told me. She claimed that she left him because she found out he was having an affair with someone from the military. She said she found a lockbox he had hidden in the closet under some other boxes, pushed way back behind some old clothes.

When she opened the box, she supposedly found letters that he had received from another man in his branch declaring his love. To this day, I don't believe that. My mom is so manipulative that I think she just came up with a reason that she thought was believable when someone asked why she left. I believe she left him because he chose to leave the military, and she was angry that she would no longer be getting his military money.

My mom told me the reason we had to leave town was that Ian was after us. According to her, our dad always had been after us but mostly Jane, and he wouldn't stop until he succeeded taking her again. Ian, apparently, had people in town watching our every move, "spying on us," as my mom would say. "They" pumped carbon monoxide into our house to kill us, although I don't remember that. Still, I don't recall a lot of things, so maybe it was true, but I always believed that it wasn't.

Imagine the scene from the movie Signs where the family was lying on the lawn; that was my mom. She went outside and lay on the lawn, rolled around, and screamed things like, "They're killing us!" My dad also "poisoned" our Kool-Aid with drugs like speed, and he would do anything to kidnap Jane again. I assumed that he wanted to kill my mom. After all, she said that people were out to get her because of him. I was so young, yet I was already living my life in fear that my mom would be killed and that I would be taken away by a stranger.

Jane must have been close to four years old when Ian first took her to New Jersey. His mom lived there so he took off to live with her. My mom told me few things about Jane's kidnapping. She said that Ian just wanted to hurt my mom, and he knew that taking Jane would do that. She also said that Ian and my uncle wanted to use Jane as their sex monkey or something like that.

On the other hand, Ian told me he never "kidnapped" Jane; he only "saved" her from our mom. At the time, our mom was in jail for writing bad checks. I didn't know that detail until he told me; my mom had kept me in the dark. Ian had told me she was on drugs all the time and drunk. He didn't want Jane to be around that, so they left the state to go to New Jersey.

My mom only conceived me because she slept with Ian again to get Jane back. As children, we are curious about how we were made or how we got to earth. I did what any kid would do, I asked my mom. She told me she slept with Ian again to trick him and get Jane back. My mom acted sweet to Ian but she didn't mean it. My mom manipulated him so she bring Jane back with her.

It wasn't a fight because I had no strength to argue. I was just so sad. My mom didn't have an ounce of emotion, other than annoyance, from my question. She created the thought in my head that I was not meant to have been born; sometimes, I even wished I never had been. I wished that I wasn't the baby who took a breath of needed air. I was blue because I had the umbilical cord around my neck, and I couldn't breathe. I blamed the doctor for saving me. It was like my mom was playing poker and had an unlucky draw. I was the joker card, but the dealer wouldn't take the card back, so she got stuck with it. Stuck with me.

When I was nineteen, I received a friend and message request on Facebook from Ian. I contemplated a few days before I decided on what do. It was as if my brain had feet and was pacing back and forth with confusion and uncertainty. I didn't want to be weak mentally, like my heart already was. Deep down, I wanted to find out why this asshole was trying to get in touch with me after so many years, so I found the courage and sent him a message on August 21, 2013. He responded the next day.

My first question to him was why. Why, after all this time, did he want to contact me. Just as my mom did, he told lies. At least, in my eyes they were lies. He told me that he'd never "stolen" Jane. He said that my mom had moved in with him and his mother, and they'd had a relationship. Not once did he tell me they were trying to conceive another child. He used the Lord to explain why they split. Everything he said caused me to have more questions about it all. Ian made it seem like he wanted to be a part of his daughters' lives but still spoke as if he wasn't sure that I was his. I didn't have enough energy, nor should I have, to prove to him that I was his daughter. It should have been him trying to show me that he cared for me just as much as he cared for Jane, but he didn't.

When I was thirteen, he came on a bus to see Jane. I waited alone in the empty room on a chair, while my mom and Jane waited at the terminal for him. When his bus pulled up, I walked to the glass door to watch. He immediately hugged Jane and then turned to my mom. The looks they exchanged with each other showed their dislike for one another. Then my mom pointed toward where I was standing, and I saw him look at me. It looked like my mom was telling him he had another daughter, but I wasn't sure why—half the time, she told me I wasn't his.

He responded by denying it. I could see his head shake. The disagreement seemed to last forever as I looked out the glass like a lost puppy.

When I asked him why he'd denied me at the bus station, he denied it as fast as he had denied me. He asked me if I remembered hugging him and asked why I would hug him if I thought he didn't claim me. At the time he had come inside, as if he wanted to rub it in my face that I wasn't his, but he put his arms out for a hug. I didn't want to hug him, but I did. I wrapped one arm around him as if I was hugging a friend from the side. When he pulled away, he told me he loved me. I just wanted to laugh, but I also wanted to cry because it was like he was toying with me.

The last message I received from Ian was him questioning if my mom told me he was my father, he added *if I was your father, then why hadn't you tried to look for me instead of partying and going out to lose your virginity.* Who the hell was he to talk to me like that?

Why did he bring up the status of my virginity; what did that have to do with him? How did he know if I had lost my virginity or not? I was utterly shocked by what I read. I knew he didn't speak to my mom about me, nor did he care to ask. He should have taken on the father role and set out to find *me,* but he didn't do that once. Ian didn't know anything about me, and it didn't seem like he wanted to know either.

Not once did he ask how I was doing. You would think after more than eighteen years, he would ask his child all about her. Ian would tell me that Jane was angry with him for not trying to communicate more. It seemed like he was annoyed at Jane for feeling upset, but how dare he think that way. This conversation was supposed to be about my life and my feelings. Did he even care that he had another daughter? It was always about Jane. I couldn't believe that was what he wanted to talk about after all this time. I figured the reason he reached out to me was to get back in contact with Jane.

They used to talk on the phone sometimes, and my mom would bitch and tell her that she didn't want Jane talking to him, but Jane always did so anyway. I suddenly got the memo that if he spoke with me, he would be able to contact Jane again. Talking to him just confused me that much more. Did he actually have a gay relationship? Did he decide that he wanted to leave the military, or did he get discharged, and why would my mom leave him if he had decided to leave the military? He would never give me straightforward answers. Instead he would be vague and go off on a tangent.

I told him that I didn't care to know what happened, but honestly, I did. I was angry and emotionally damaged with what he said; I didn't want him believing that he had affected me. All those years, he made me feel so small and insignificant, but I couldn't let him know those feelings bothered me. I wasn't about to play his twisted mind game with him.

After our conversation, I was more confused than ever. What was I to believe now? Ian claimed that it was my mom who had kidnapped Jane, but she had always told me it was him. So, was she the one who was lying? She also never told me that she was in New Jersey for a long period. Ian had made it seem like she was living her life with him and his mom, as a family. According to her, she only went there to get Jane back. Nothing made sense anymore, not that it ever had. Trying to listen to both sides of the story made me feel like I was sitting in the front row of a presidential debate that never ended. Even now, it gives me a migraine to think about it.

Nick also referred to Ian as his 'sperm-donor' because Ian wasn't a present father figure in Nick's life. All Ian did was help bring him into this world. Nick told me stories about Ian's life experiences that my mom had never told me. What exactly was she keeping from me? Better yet, why was she hiding information from me?

On February 26, 2016, I reached out to Ian. Three years had passed, and I couldn't stop thinking about all the questions that were still unanswered. It haunted me to know the truth. I wanted and needed to know what the truth was. I sat down on my bed, anxiously trying to figure out what to say to him. My heart was beating so fast that it felt like I was just a few pulses away from passing out. I stared blankly at my phone as my fingers started moving on their own. My heart and mind were speaking to my hands as I typed this message: "Are you there?"

Quickly Ian replied with, "Why?"

That was not the response I thought he would give. He should have been excited that I'd contacted him again, but he just questioned my intentions. My eyes immediately rolled as I took a deep breath and tried to explain to him that I would like it if we could get to know one another.

One of us had to swallow our pride and say it. Obviously, it wasn't going to be Ian, so I had to do it. We chatted back and forth like awkward acquaintances. It was like I was at the mall and saw one of my classmates. I tried to avoid that classmate by hiding behind the clothing racks, but we ended up running into each other, so I got stuck in a conversation that neither of us wanted to be a part of. That's how I felt with him, like neither of us truly wanted to be in conversation.

It seemed to be small talk at first. He would say things like, "Hope you have a good day. You deserve it." Then it happened. This man I didn't even know said it again; Ian dared to say, "I love you." At first, the shock took over my body, but then I was overwhelmed with rage. This man didn't even know my middle name, let alone my age, but somehow, he loved me? He was the mastermind of my confusion.

I tried to look on the bright side and just be happy that I was finally building a relationship with him. My gut had been giving me different signals, ever since I hit *send* that first time. There was so much hope and wishful thinking in building just a friendship with him that I pushed the deranged parts of what he would tell me to the side, just like he did to my mom and me.

At first, our conversations seemed headed in the right direction, but it started to go downhill at a fast pace when Ian got extremely needy and started messaging me excessively every day. If you're familiar with Facebook, you know that it shows when someone is typing a message. When I would start typing, I would see the notification pop up that he was typing too, but he would stop showing he was typing when I stopped. As soon as I started typing again, he also started typing. Then, a few seconds or minutes would pass before he messaged again.

If I didn't respond quickly enough, he would ask what I was doing and why it was more important than talking to him. Ian played the victim card as if we were playing poker, over and over, and sadly, it was working. I felt pitiful for how mean I was to him three years ago. I gave him the benefit of the doubt; after all, he had reached out first.

My mom always played the victim card, and I let her make me feel guilty because she was my mom. I believed that's how I was supposed to feel because that's what I was shown and taught. To my knowledge, everyone's parents acted the same. Ian was my biological father, so I should treat him with the same respect that I did for my mom. They both knew I was naive and vulnerable enough to always to come back and apologize that I was wrong, even if I was right.

At one point, Ian would say things to hold me liable for everything that had happened. He never blatantly said those words, but still beat around the bush. One minute, he would say something like, "Hello, dear," and if I didn't respond within two seconds, he would say that I was hardly on Messenger or that I wasn't talking to him again. It was so frustrating because I was working my ass off with two jobs—three, if you count my promotional modeling jobs—and if I had free time, I enjoyed spending time with my friends or running errands. He gave me his number and said he'd like to hear my voice.

A phone call seemed nice and somewhat genuine, but I was immediately let down again. Just like on Messenger, I could barely get a word in. Ian would talk only about himself—how my mom ruined everything in his life—and he kept asking about my sister, Jane. He wouldn't accept the fact that I didn't know much about her. We weren't that close, and I didn't talk to her. In his mind, she was the angel child, and he put her on a high pedestal so there should be no reason why I didn't talk to her. I got tired of him calling her "Jane-baby". I would try to tell him *why* I didn't talk to her, but it was in one ear and out the other. He wouldn't accept that I didn't know about her personal life. I knew my sister's personality, and she was far from the picture he had of her in his head.

Not once did he ever take responsibility for any part—or lack of part—that he had played in my mom's life and mine. Instead, Ian singled out my mom for all the situations that had turned out bad. According to him, the Lord Almighty would take care of her when the time came. Since he asked for forgiveness for everything he'd done wrong in his life, he was automatically in the clear. I felt like I was talking to my mom because she would say the same kind of crap. After all, he was the Lord's "special" child, as my mom was too.

What a load of shit! Ian even had the nerve to take credit for where I was in my life. The reason for my success, he said, was because I came from him, so he had helped. How dare he! How dare he try to say he helped me in any way. I was successful because of *me*. But he said I woke up every day because of him. I had the will to live because of him. Little did he know that I barely had that will to live, and he was at fault for that partially. The last thing I did before shutting my eyes to drift off to sleep was think of him. He wished I thought about him that often.

One day, I finally snapped from extreme annoyance. I told him that until he stopped bringing the Lord into every sentence and taking credit for my life, he could stop talking to me. This guy had so many tricks up his sleeve and knew how to guilt me into keep talking to him. He could have been a magician, pulling a bunny from a hat, because he was so good at fooling me. After all, I was an easy target for guilt-tripping. It was like I had a big bull's-eye on my chest.

He kept explaining that he didn't take credit for everything, but I wouldn't be on this earth if it weren't for him. Apparently, every time I looked in the mirror, I should see him because we were the "same." I didn't even know what he looked like. Even though he wasn't with me physically, he was in spirit, he said. Bullshit! He was one of the main reasons I was so fucked up.

A couple of months had passed, and I started to see the crazy that Nick had explained to me. Here was this man, snaking his way back into my life, and I let it happen. Ian always had something going on in his life, but they were more like fictional stories. He was like the man from the movie *Big Fish*. The newest story he had to tell me was that a woman in London had left him millions of dollars in her will. Of course, when I would ask him why she chose him or how he knew her, he jumped around my question. I knew he was lying.

He was full of stories, like a book that had no ending. Every day, I would get a message from him about the check he would soon be receiving and that he would be rich. Ian even asked me to go to London with him, and when I declined, he couldn't understand why. In his eyes he was my dad. Never in a million years would I even go to another state, let alone another country, with a man I had only met once, whether he was my dad. Being my biological father didn't make him the oh-so-holy person he pretended to be. He asked me if he should go straight to Italy to get his car or stop to see me. Yeah, it would have been so cool if it were true, but it wasn't. I knew he wasn't going to get a check or a car—or come to see me.

At some point during all this mess, he had an epiphany that he wasn't getting this imaginary check. It was like he was waiting for rain in the Sahara Desert or snow fall in Death Valley. Can you guess what he did next? Yes, he came up with a new lie. Ian told me there was a different check coming from someone else in London. Of course, he still ignored every question I threw at him and always asked why I was questioning him. Kids normally asked for help from their parents, right? It shouldn't be the other way around, but this sorry excuse for a man had the nerve to ask me for $350.

Ian explained that it was the fee that Western Union wanted before they would release the check to him. I told him I didn't have the money, and even if I did, I wouldn't give someone I didn't know well enough that much. He said the banker was sweet on him so he would have her pay it, and then he'd repay her with $20,000. It was like he was using the made-up banker to make me feel bad for not helping him.

He must be telling the truth like everything else that came out of his mouth, right? No! These crazy types of messages kept coming for months. Notification after notification. He stopped asking about me and my life once again. He never asked how I was doing or how I was feeling. The conversations were all about him, just like they had been in the beginning, and he always reminded me of how my mom screwed everything up. God had made a clone of my mom and thought the world needed a male version.

Ian didn't give me a chance to respond to his messages. He would send one message; then, not even a second later, I would get another. Every one of them had the same timestamp next to it. It was like he had his messages already typed out, stored in a 'For a Rainy Day' folder, and he just needed to copy and paste them. Each message got progressively meaner than the last. He was aggressively asking me where I was and why I hadn't responded yet. There was nothing in my life as important as him. Again, this was what my mom would do too, if I didn't respond quickly enough to her texts.

I would tell Ian I was working or with a friend, and he would say things to make me feel bad because they had my attention instead of him. Nothing I said to him was a good enough response. What the fuck? A stranger was expecting me to drop everything for him, yet he never did for me, ever, in my twenty-one years of life. Somehow, he managed to get inside my head and make me feel like it was my fault that my mom left and didn't tell him about me.

Why did he think it was her responsibility to tell him about me or that she had gotten pregnant? If it was true that she was living with him at his mom's in New Jersey, then he would have known she was pregnant. My mom said that she *did* tell him, but he always denied that I was his. He would make excuses, such as saying that I was black so I couldn't be his child. I let him make me feel like garbage because I cared. I've often asked myself what is wrong with me and what I ever did to deserve this shit. *Why are you so weak?* I'd think.

Ian was starting to brainwash me into thinking he actually cared about me because he was staying in contact. I wasn't that important to him however, and I learned that later on. He was very good at letting me know he cared about Jane, though. She was his baby, as he would say, like a parent does when he's bragging on his child. I couldn't wrap my mind around it. All this time, the sole reason for his finding me was so he could find Jane again. He wanted me to get them in contact with each other, like old times. I told him countless times that I didn't have a relationship with her because my mom had control over her. She wasn't the same Jane I once knew when we were younger.

Ian couldn't understand, and he wouldn't try to. In one of his messages, he asked what I was doing, I said I was going to the gym, and his response was, "Good, you need to go to the gym." What did he mean by that? If it was supposed to be an offhand comment, it didn't seem like it. It felt more like a rude jab at my insecurities. He often hurt feelings. I couldn't get anywhere with him, and I wasn't learning anything new about him either.

Our conversations got more annoying. They never changed, and there was only so much I could take of hearing about his "awful" life. He wore me down with seemingly endless and draining conversations.

Finally, I stopped responding. The messages from him slowed. I got a new message notification from him about once a month, but I didn't open them. If the internet could grow dust, the messages would have been covered with grime. I even created a new Facebook account to avoid contact with him.

I didn't feel any sadness or guilt this time. It was almost like a weight had been lifted off my shoulders when I stopped contact with Ian. Sometimes, I will log into my old Facebook account to see the last message next to his name to see if I have any emotions, but I don't have any. I'm not sad that I lost him. I couldn't lose something I never had anyway.

Ian,

I feel bad for you. I pity you. I wish I could have learned to love you, but you made that almost impossible. You'll always be a distant memory. I used to wish I knew you, but I don't feel that way anymore. It's your loss, not mine. I want you to know that I continued living without you, and I made it to where I am without your help because you never did help me. I sometimes wonder about your well-being, but I don't allow it to bother me because I doubt you ever wonder about me. I learned to be strong; I just never thought I would have to be strong enough to shield my own heart from the man who was supposed to be my father. I don't hate you because I can't. I hope you can help yourself one day.

CHAPTER THREE

---

sis·ter

/ˈsistər/

noun
a woman or girl in relation to other daughters and sons of her parents

Just like any other siblings, my sister Jane and I fought. Jane thought I was the brattiest little sister, and I thought she was the meanest older sister. She would always say that the three-and-a-half-year age gap gave her the power to act like a dick. We couldn't stand each other, and I wished I had a different sister, but deep down we loved each other. We just weren't good at showing it.

She would do anything for me, though. If you messed with me, you messed with her. If I got bullied, and she found out who it was, she would make that person's life a living hell. She always said, "That's my sister! If I want to be mean to her, I can, because she's my little sister, but you can't." She was like the big brother I never had sometimes.

I was always getting hurt somehow, and water, especially, didn't seem to like me. My cousin, my sister, and I were at a neighbor's abandoned house, catching frogs in the pool. The shallow end only had muddy puddles, but the deep end had green algae-infested water. It reminded me of a perfect home for a swamp monster. We had a small bucket to collect the frogs in. Each time one of us got one, we would pluck it up by its long leg and toss it into the bucket. We made it into a game to see who could get the most frogs, and since I was so competitive, I wanted to win. When I went to catch the little frog, it jumped away, and I slipped in a puddle.

I flailed my arms around, but there was nothing to grasp, and I slid into the deep end to where I couldn't touch the bottom. I felt myself falling, but there was nothing I could do. Before I could even scream, I was head deep in the monster's territory. I was frantically splashing, with my head bobbing in and out of the water. My heart continued to beat out of my chest

every time I came back up for air. My eyes were searching everywhere for anything that could help me. My
cousin was pacing up and down the side of the pool.
He couldn't reach me because I was in the middle and
just kept going farther out.

Jane dumped the bucket of frogs we had spent so
much time catching and found some fishing line. I
was almost more upset about losing our frogs, than
being concerned about being saved. She tied it in a
knot around the bucket and threw it out to me. My
arms reached out for it, but I kept going under the
dark-green water. The bucket just floated above me,
bobbing up and down. Jane was screaming for me.
Her words sounded as if she was inside a bubble, like
she was so far away from me. *"Elle!"* My name didn't
sound like my name after a while. I could almost feel
her fear; it was so strong. I was fading in and out. I
could no longer hear anything but the sound of water
filling up my ears and flooding my head.

Jane pulled the bucket back and, with all her might,
threw it out to me again. Somehow, I used all the
strength I had left and finally grabbed on. She started
pulling me in, but the line broke, and I went back
under the water. When I came back up, I managed to
push the bucket back toward her.

She was yelling at our cousin to help because she was getting more terrified as the seconds ticked by. At that point, I didn't know how scared I was anymore. My mind decided to give up. I thought, okay, *it's my time to die, I guess* and I was okay with dying in that moment. I felt my lungs slowly filling with more water and green goop. Jane then tied the line again but this time with five knots, and she slung it out again. I grabbed on, and she started pulling. I kicked with my feet as hard as I could, but it felt like I was going nowhere.

My body was losing energy, and my lungs felt nearly full of water. They felt like they were practically floating inside my body, but as much as I wanted to give up, I didn't, and neither did Jane. She wasn't going to let me give up. My cousin and Jane both grabbed my hands and hoisted me up from the water. I couldn't stand; my feet had become mushy, and my legs just sank to the ground. I started coughing up the green water as they picked me up and carried me next door to my mom. Jane didn't want to let go of me. She whispered in my ear, just before I lost consciousness, "Don't ever do that again. I can't lose you." I miss that sister who cared for me.

The older I got, the meaner she seemed to be. I

always tried to remember the Jane who had saved my life and replace her with the one who was hateful now. She did her best to protect me from other people, but it was a different story for her. If I was sitting in her spot on the couch or in her room, she would physically beat me until I was screaming and calling for Mark. He was like a best friend—my dad. He loved me like I was his flesh and blood, and Jane was envious. I was a tattler and seemed to love to get her in trouble.

Mark would yell at her and spank her—back then, it was socially acceptable to spank your kids. I could hear her crying and yelling from the other room. The belt scared her but not enough because she still mistreated me. When one person borrows your stuff without asking, there will most likely be a fight. She was a bit excessive. She put locks on her door and told me she would kill me if I ever stepped one foot through her bedroom door. Maybe that was the reason why I woke up with a knife under my pillow. When I was younger, I sleepwalked, and I would grab a knife—subconsciously I felt the need to protect myself.

Jane also hated it if I looked at her. She'd sit across from me, and if she saw that I looked her way, within seconds she was on top of me, punching and screaming, "Don't ever look at me again!" It was like I was the helpless zebra, and she was a big lion without pity.

Mark pulled her off me and pulled out the belt then started swinging at her butt. Behind the tears streaming down her face, she mouthed, *I hate you.* Yeah, I was bratty and annoying, but I didn't understand why she hated me so much. What did I do to deserve that much hatred? I stopped trying to go everywhere she went, and I stopped talking to her. Jane quit walking me to my bus stop, and I stopped caring. She was the troubled child, and I was the angel who could do no wrong in my parents' eyes.

When Jane was in eighth grade, our mom found a notebook with her 'sex list.' She was only fourteen— she had failed a grade—and already had sex with about twelve people. A couple of people on that list were girls. Our mom was extremely disappointed in her, but Jane said it was her body, and she would do what she wanted with it.

Back when Myspace was the trendy social media, I was scrolling through it and came across pictures of Jane in lingerie. The kind of lingerie you would see in a *Playboy* magazine. She posted a picture of her lips and captioned it, "Look at those DSL's." I googled 'What is a DSL?' I found out it meant 'dick-sucking lips,' I was mortified and so disgusted.

The first thing I did was holler for my mom, and, of course, I snitched. Jane got grounded to her room for the weekend. Black-and-blue bruises covered my body; I could have tasted all the blood if it weren't dried next to my lip. Jane really pummeled me. I was tired of being her punching bag, so I stood up for myself the next time she hit me. My fist made its way to her jaw, and I hit her back hard; that was the last time she put her hands on me.

I avoided her like she was anthrax until I was about fourteen because I was over her antics. Since she was almost eighteen, she had more important things on her mind instead of me, like sex and drugs. If she didn't sneak out with her friends, we would talk occasionally. She had her friends, and I had mine. Jane eventually stopped trying to run all my friends off or steal them away from me.

Soon, I became her personal diary. Every day was a new entry about what pill she had popped, who she had fucked that week, or where she was going to sneak off next. She told me that she had gone to Schwag-fest (a big hippie event) with some of her friends and a few people she didn't even know. She said she'd smoked marijuana and that she had experienced mushrooms, which, she said they had made her go on a psychedelic trip. Time moved so slow-ly and she felt like she was floating through everyone. She told me how much fun it had been, but it didn't sound like even a teeny bit of fun to me.

She didn't sound like the sister I knew, and I was disappointed in her. I loved that I had my sister again. I didn't want to ruin it so I decided to shut my mouth, lock it, and throw away the key.

I didn't realize that having her as my sister wasn't a good thing until I got to middle school. Jane had an unfortunate reputation and little did I know that I would be held to the same standard. The only benefit of Jane being my sister was that everyone was afraid of me because they all saw her as a threat. If she wasn't busy sleeping with someone's boyfriend, then she was fighting their girlfriend. It didn't matter if you were a male or a female; she would hit you, regardless. She was like the Ronda Rousey before the fight with Amanda Nunes: undefeated and without fear.

Jane couldn't hold down a job for the life of her. She just wasn't good at focusing or concentrating on any-thing that wasn't about her. For whatever reason, she wanted everything handed to her without earning it. It seemed like our mom was the same way. She became a stripper as soon as she turned eighteen and as shocking as it seems, she was damn good at it. I only assume she was because she was, metaphorically speaking, rolling in money. It made me sad that she thought the only thing she was good at was showing her body for money. She didn't know her worth. Sometimes, I would see her cry late at night or hear her tell Mark how awful her night was when we picked her up from the club. I could see the shame on her face some nights when she walked through the door to her room.

She was so pretty that she could have done modeling instead of wearing skimpy clothes while grinding on the grimy pole for a measly dollar. Being a stripper had changed her once again. The diary entries had slowed, and the only time I could get her to hang out with me was when I sat in the living room while she straightened or curled her long, bleached hair. Her beauty had me in awe.

The house across the street came up for rent, and she pounced on it like a cat with a mouse. She wanted it, and she didn't stop until she got it. Jane was that way with anything; she always had a way of getting whatever she wanted. The guy who moved in with her seemed sketchy to me. He practically never slept, and different cars came and went at all times of the day and night. I didn't know that he was a drug dealer, and I don't think she knew that either when she told him he could move in with her. I would sit in our living room, watching her house across the street through our big picture window.

When it was dark, all I could see was her little porch light flickering as her roommate stepped outside to hand something to the person at the bottom of the steps. It happened quickly, and within moments, the car sped down the street in the other direction. When I went over to the house, there would be weed, pipes, and Jane's bong sitting on the coffee table in plain sight. I was afraid of something bad happening, like a robbery or a shoot-out, because of her roommate's drug dealing. I tried to let her know I was there if she needed me, just by going over to her house to spend time with her and play Guitar Hero.

They always had parties, and when I would cross paths with Jane, she looked sickly. Our mom and Mark intervened and told her she needed to kick her roommate to the curb. It was like Jane was afraid of him because it took Mark being with her for her to confront him.

When her roommate moved out, he left a lot of

shit there, so we had to help her get rid of it. When we picked up the cushions from his couch, we found a few bags of weed. Mark reached his hand inside a hole in the bottom of the couch and pulled out a bag of something white. We assumed it was cocaine.

When I looked at my sister, all I felt was sadness. This new life she was living had changed her. I didn't know if she was doing drugs or dealing, but I just hoped she wasn't. At one point, we had been so close, but now it was like she was on her own island, and I just had to float way out to the sea to watch from a distance. I didn't know who she was anymore.

We found out that her roommate had been stripping copper wires and selling them. There were bundles of them in the garage, rolled up like hay bales and shoved under dusty blue tarps. Jane didn't live in the house for long after he left because she couldn't afford it on her own. Soon, she was back with us. Shortly afterward she started dating a guy she'd gone to high school with, and then she moved in with him and his mom. She seemed genuinely happy. They threw a party one night and invited me, and she swore she wouldn't tell Mom. I believed her so I drank and danced all night long with my boyfriend.

She lied to me, though, because the very next day

my mom grounded me. She was furious, and Mark was disappointed. I was so enraged with Jane that I told her she could jump off a cliff, and I wouldn't even bat an eyelash. I'd kept all of her secrets boxed up and hidden from our mom, yet she couldn't keep any of my secrets, even the one she had created for me.

Jane got pregnant, and she confided in me. At that point, she had pushed me over the edge, and all the buttons she pressed were lit up. I didn't give a damn about what was going on with her. I thought, *It doesn't surprise me one bit because she's always sleeping around.*

I insisted that she tell Mom because she would find out anyway when Jane started showing, and I was tired of holding all her secrets for her. I felt she was using me as her guinea pig. My mom and Mark didn't find out about her pregnancy until Jane called, bawling her eyes out, screaming, "Something is wrong! I'm bleeding!" We sped over to her boyfriend's house and saw that she had lost the baby. It was so sad, seeing her hold the Ziploc with blood inside of it. Even though I was so mad at her, it pained me to see her so sad. It wasn't even a baby yet, just a small sac, and she was devastated.

She and her boyfriend broke up shortly after that, and once again, she moved back in with us. We didn't talk as we had before. I kept to myself, mostly because I was tired of her burning our bridges to each other. She kept to herself when he was home.

One day, she came home with a guy and introduced him as her new boyfriend. His name was Carlos. He was about six feet tall, with tattoos from his head to his toes. His neck was tattooed with random words and symbols, and he had more than one swastika. It amused me a bit because my mom was Jewish, and here was Jane, with a guy who had anti-Jewish markings. He had spider webs on both of his elbows, which, I eventually learned was for his being trapped and 'tangled up in the prison system'. At least that's what my friends told me it meant.

Jane looked even happier than she was with the last guy. It felt like only a month had passed when she told us they were moving into a townhouse together.

At first, I wasn't sure about him. He seemed dangerous because he was in a gang and had been to jail several times, but he was actually like a big, sweet teddy bear. We became extremely close; he was like a brother to me. Jane was still stripping. She insisted on going to the beauty store to get CHI hair products. Carlos invited me to go along with them every time because he didn't like to go in the store with her. Once we dropped her off, I would climb over the middle console to the front seat of the Corvette, and then we would get Frappuccino's from the coffee shop in the parking lot. Carlos would always roll up the window and catch my hair in it, and we both laughed as he held the button up to keep me from rolling it back down to release the strands of hair that were caught between the glass and door frame.

The seasons changed so fast. Leaves fell; snow drifted down then melted. Spring came and went then summer hit. Jane and Carlos were still together, and he was like a brother to me. Jane, however, was extremely jealous and even accused me of sleeping with him. It was absolutely ridiculous because I would never do that.

One day, Jane came rushing over to our house, excited. She yelled at the top of her lungs that they were engaged and beamed with excitement. We could practically see the happiness shining off her skin. I was happy too. Carlos and I had become so close, and I was excited that he was going to become my brother in-law. (Now that I'm older, I don't really know if he had proposed to her.) That night, Jane asked Mark to go to the store with her to get some groceries and items for the townhouse, and I joined them. While riding there, my face was buried in a book; I couldn't take my eyes off the pages. I had to keep reading, as if the words would disappear. When we got to the store, I begged Mark to let me stay in the car so I could read. I used the light from my phone to illuminate the pages because it was dark outside.

I was in a trance, reading, when there was a tap on the window. I nearly jumped out of my skin. It was a man in black. With him were a couple of other men in two cars with blacked-out windows; they were angled to block in Mark's car. The men had their spotlights beamed at our car. *Terrified* doesn't even describe what I was feeling. The man asked if I was Elle and then asked me to step out of the car. I hesitated because I didn't know him.

He sensed my fear and flashed his badge. He explained he was an officer from Texas and was searching for Carlos. I called Mark's phone and told them to come outside immediately. I saw a look of shock on Jane's face as she walked toward the car. The world stopped time for a moment; it felt like the earth was still. Everything went silent. Even the sound of cars passing, and onlookers whispering had fallen quiet.

I could feel sweat rolling down my forehead, seemingly in slow motion, and I could practically feel heat radiating from Jane. My heart seemed to be beating out of my chest, and my hands became clammy. The officer told Jane to slide in the front seat of one of the cop cars. Mark was just as confused as I was. There was something she was keeping from us, but what was it?

I knew it was something bad because I saw Jane crying through the windshield of the car she was in. Her tears glistened from the spotlights around the vehicles in the parking lot. Time was ticking. Jane shook her head a few times and then nodded, as if agreeing. She quickly stepped out of the car, and the two cars sped off.

We could barely make out the words Jane said, but eventually, we learned that Carlos was being arrested. He had robbed a grocery store at gunpoint and then fled the scene is what she told us. The state had been looking for him for some time. They finally traced him back to Oklahoma.

My thoughts were in a whirlwind, and my head was spinning. Carlos had become like my brother, and now he was being ripped away from me—from all of us.

Jane wrote letters to him in prison, and he wrote back every time, so I started writing to him too. She told him she would wait for him, but her letters to him eventually became less frequent, as did the letters from him. I still remember the sadness and pain I felt when Carlos wrote to me and told me that they broke off their relationship. She had explained that it was too hard, being so far away and being so lonely. There was more to it, but he didn't tell me until years later. The truth was that Jane and Carlos had lost whatever feelings they had for one another. He said it was mostly just physical between them since day one anyway. Carlos and I kept in contact for a year, and then, I thought he must have been moved to a different prison because I stopped receiving letters from him. I was devastated. I tried to find him, but I couldn't. I never wrote to him again.

Months passed by, and my sister was still torn up. When she found out I had been writing to Carlos, she accused me of trying to be with him again. I was grossed out because he was truly like my brother, but she didn't believe me. She started dating another guy she had gone to school with. I wasn't surprised at that point because she was like the Energizer bunny, hopping from one guy to the next.

One day, she came to have lunch with Mom and me. She told us she had news. Jane was pregnant again, but this time she was two months along, and the doctors said everything was going great. My mom was happy for her, and Jane was happy again, so it made me happy too.

Jane had stopped doing hard drugs but couldn't put down the weed or cigarettes. Our mom blamed her boyfriend Joseph for it. She said he was drugging Jane and trying to kill her. Mom also said that she could see the white powdery substance at the bottom of the cigarette boxes.

There was no way I believed that because they were so happy together.

Joseph had been in the same grade at school as Jane. They had classes together through high school, although they never dated. Joseph played football, and he was great at it. I had a feeling she tried to get his attention back then, but it didn't work. They made such a cute couple. They were always laughing and being playful together, and they included my boyfriend and me in so many things. We went to Joseph's mom's house, where Jane was living, and we all played Apples to Apples then went outside and tossed a football. Everything seemed perfect for Jane and Joseph.

When Jane was about six months pregnant, she moved back in with us. I was confused about that, and when I asked my mom, she said that Jane wanted to come home and be with family. We went to pick her up, and when we got to Joseph's house, my mom told Mark and me to stay in the car. She walked quickly to the door, as if she was in a hurry, and I heard her call out. The door opened, and Jane came out, holding a box of her things; my mom was clutching Jane's arm. Joseph stood on the porch, pleading with my mom not to take her. They got into the car, and as we drove away, I looked back at Joseph. He had his face in his hands and seemed to be crying.

I later found out that it was Mom who convinced Jane that she would need her help with the baby. The last few months of her pregnancy flew by. She didn't have bad mood swings, and she seemed to be very content, for the most part. She was good at making it seem like she was okay, but I knew she was hurting from not being able to see or talk to Joseph. She still had some things at his house. It seemed he was holding on-to them in the hope that she would come back to him, but my mom threatened that all hell would break lose if he didn't bring her stuff to our house.

He brought her things to over, and my mom was at the door waiting for him. He left our house that day without seeing or speaking to Jane. He was in tears—broken and upset. He called almost every day, but my mom wouldn't let them talk. Jane started to plead every time the phone rang, but my mom always said no and told her that he would just hurt her, even though it was my mom causing the pain. He left messages on the answering machine every time he called. I could hear the pain in his words and the crackle his voice would make when he said that he loved Jane. I was so depressed for her but especially for him.

Mom didn't seem to care that she was hurting Jane. Even Mark wasn't sure what to do. He reached out to Joseph and gave updates on how Jane was doing. He told Joseph that Jane missed and loved him just as much as he did her. I hated our mom for what she was doing. It wasn't fair. There were only a few days before Jane's due date, and Joseph knew it. He called twice a day, begging to be there for his daughter's birth. The day Jane went into labor, Joseph wasn't there, not because he didn't want to be but because my mom kept the information from him. He didn't know which hospital she was in, so he missed seeing his daughter's birth.

Joseph fell back into drugs and stopped taking care of himself. It drove him crazy. He was sent to jail, off and on, and then would be put in the hospital for mental illness for weeks at a time. He eventually was diagnosed with schizophrenia. He fell down the rabbit hole because of the pain my mom caused him.

Back when Jane moved back in with us, before she had her baby, Joseph had gotten an apartment of his own, but his behavior drastically changed soon after, and he was forced to move into a mental health clinic. He once thought that I was my sister and started telling me how much he loved me (Jane).

I can't imagine what it must be like to not see your child when the they are born then have the love of your life ripped away from you. It undoubtedly changed him. Joseph missed out on the birth of his beautiful daughter, but he has been getting better every day and continuing to work on himself, all for Emma.

Jane,

I wish I could have known how this life was going to turn out. We had such a bipolar relationship, the epitome of love and hate, but I have always loved you far more than I could have ever hated you. I miss you. I miss our fights and how we would make up just by giving each other "the look" of being okay. I often think about the good times we had, like when we went to the mall during Christmas, got those quarter-machine mustaches, and wore them throughout the mall. It entertained us when people laughed. Then we took a picture with Santa, and you wrote "We're Jews" on a piece of paper, right before they took the picture. We laughed so hard and didn't care about the snickers we got from anyone around us. We were together, having fun, and that's all that mattered. I even lied to you when I said I liked the Nike's you bought us that matched. They were hideous, but I loved that you wanted to have something the same with me. I miss when we would fight over who got to sing Nat King Cole on that tiny karaoke machine.

I'm sorry I didn't try hard enough to help you before it was too late. I wish you would have listened to me when I told you not to move back in with us. At the time, it seemed like it was just because I didn't want you there, but I always had a bad feeling. I never agreed with Mom for keeping you and Joseph apart. I'm also sorry I never told you how much you mean to me. I love you so much, and I will always be here for you. I won't rush you to be okay. I will never give up on you either. You're not alone, and you never will be. I know that what you're going through must be so hard, and I could never imagine what it's like. Whenever you're ready, just tell me, and I'll be there.

Your little sister,

Elle

CHAPTER FOUR

———

niece

/nēs/

noun

a daughter of one's brother or sister, or
one's brother-in-law or sister-in-law

I was staying with my other sister, Hanna, for a few
weeks in Illinois when my mom called.

"Jane is in labor, and Emma will be here any minute!" she shouted with excitement.

I was so thrilled but also a bit nervous for Jane. My
gut churned because I knew how our mom got when
she went to the doctor with us. My mom always told
the nurses that she knew everything. When we were
kids, Mom would tell us that the doctor didn't know
what he (or she) was talking about when the doctor left

the room. She always made it a point to be smarter and better than anyone else.

I don't know why she believed she was better than others. When the nurse would come into the room to inform us of what the doctor said or what we needed to do, my mom would say that she already knew. Every time, the nurses were annoyed but they plastered a smile on their faces as my mom spoke. I imagined them walking out of the room, rolling their eyes, and mumbling cuss words because I was doing the same thing.

I felt bad for leaving Hanna without saying good-bye, but I wanted to be there for Jane and her baby, Emma. I got in my car immediately, sped to the gas station to fill up, and made the long ten-hour drive to Oklahoma. To my surprise, I didn't get pulled over, even though I was flying down the highway. If I blinked, I would have missed the road signs—at least, it felt like I was going that fast.

When I had arrived, I had to go in circles and up and down the rows in the parking lot to find a spot that wasn't in another country away from the door. My tires squealed as I whipped into a free spot. I jumped out of my car, slammed the door, and sprinted inside. Luckily, my mom had told me which room they were in because the receptionist wouldn't have been able to understand me; I was out of breath and in a jumbled headspace.

This was my first niece from Jane, and the first one I would get to see the day she was born. I was incredibly thrilled. Everything seemed to be taking a long time. The elevator was full the first time, so I had to wait for the next one before I could go to the third floor.

I shuffled on either foot as I debated whether to run up the stairs, but the elevator dinged to go up as I turned to bolt to the stairs. I hurried into the empty elevator and repeatedly pushed the *close* button so no one else could get on. No one else in the hospital seemed to need to get anywhere. If I could have grown facial hair, I would have had a beard by the time I made it to her room.

Emma was born three hours before I got there. She was eight pounds of perfect. I had never seen Jane look at anything with as much love as she looked at her baby. Then there was our mom, acting as if she was the one who had delivered her. She said that she had to help coach the doctor throughout the whole delivery. I rolled my eyes and took a deep breath to keep from telling her to shut up because that would have started a fight. My sister looked so tired as she held her baby, but she couldn't seem to take her eyes off her.

Mom took Emma out of my sisters' arms and told her she needed to rest. Emma started screaming and waving her tiny arms. I reached out for her, and she reached toward me. My mom seemed irritated that Emma wanted me and not her, but I didn't care. I was in love. My niece was the most beautiful thing I had seen. We rocked back and forth until she stopped crying. She was in my arms for almost thirty minutes before I realized I needed to eat something. Holding her close to my chest, I kissed her forehead, got up, and handed her back to Jane. I gave Emma one last touch, and before I lifted my hand, she wrapped her sweet tiny pinky around mine.

Over the next few weeks, anywhere I was, so was Emma. No matter what I was doing, I was holding her. This little baby had the biggest piece of my heart, and I could see the joy radiating off Jane. I could tell that she was so proud of the sweet baby she'd helped create. Mark admired Emma too. If she wasn't with Jane or me, she was with Mark.

My mom was busy trying to control everything, as always. She told Jane she wasn't allowed to hang out with anyone or leave the house without telling her where she was going. Jane was twenty-four but Mom treated her like a child. The arguments got worse between her and Mom. I didn't live with them so when I wasn't working, I was at Mark's house. He lived next door to Mom and Jane. Sometimes, I tried to stay at my mom's and play with Emma to keep her away from the arguing, and if it escalated, I would take her over to Mark's; she didn't need to be around that.

My mom called me when I was at Mark's and said she wanted me to take her to the department store. Mark said he would come too. When I opened the door at Mom's house, I heard Emma squeal and saw her pull herself up. She used the couch cushion to help guide her as she stumbled to me.

"Are you ready to go on a ride?" I said to her, and she grinned.

I didn't see Jane but didn't think anything of it. She might have been asleep.

Later, at the store, my mom's phone started ringing repeatedly. She finally answered but didn't even say hello before Jane started shouting, so loudly, that Mark and I could hear her. "Where the fuck did you take my baby?" I'm pretty sure everyone near us heard it too.

My mom kept her voice calm and told her we were at the store, "We're just paying and will be home soon."

I was embarrassed, and I think Mark was too.

When we pulled into the driveway, Jane ran toward us. She was fuming with anger. Her face was beet red, and her eyes were wet with tears. Mark grabbed some bags to help my mom, but I grabbed Emma's car seat. I didn't want her in the line of fire. We walked to my mom's, all while Jane and Mom were screaming at each other. The front door was wide open, and when I stepped over the threshold, I could see that the back door was open too. It was barely hanging on its hinges because Jane had broken the door to get inside. I learned that the reason I hadn't seen her when I first got there was that she was at the neighbor's house. My mom locked her out because she had disobeyed her. Mom never gave Jane a key because she needed to control who Jane brought over and where she was at all times.

I stood by the door with Emma, still in her car seat, and Mark stood in the doorway, looking in. Mom and Jane were in the kitchen, yelling and throwing stuff at each other. Mark and I spoke with our eyes, and I started toward the door, planning to take Emma to his place.

Jane was hot on my tracks and spun me around. Her grip was tight on my shoulder as she said, "Where do you think you're taking my baby?"

"Emma doesn't need to be around your fighting." I kept my voice calm because I didn't want to upset Emma anymore than she already was. Jane obviously thought differently; she yanked the car seat from my hand. Emma started shrieking. Jane shoved me back, but this time I didn't back down like I had when we were kids.

I stepped right up to her. My face was so close that our noses were practically touching. Angry tears filled behind my eyes. I'd had enough of her bullshit. My heart was pounding like I'd just run a 5K marathon. I clenched my jaw but then calmly said, "Jane, get out of my way and let me take Emma to Mark's house."

Jane sat the car seat down, not so gently, and then threatened me and pushed me back.

With anger and fury in my eyes, I snapped, "I'm not afraid of you anymore. The only reason I'm not beating your ass right now is because of that little girl!" as I pointed towards Emma.

Mark reached for my arm "We need to go to my place."

We didn't even make it into his living room before we heard the yelling start up again. It felt like my heart was stabbed every time Emma's cries got louder. I couldn't take it anymore, so I dialed 911. If I couldn't stop them from fighting, I knew the cops would. I'm sure they were tired of coming out to my mom's. They were there at least three times that week, and the last time was because my mom called them on Jane. Jane had pulled a knife on Mom—that's what Mom had said—and had threatened to stab her.

Usually, cops take a long time to show up, but they got there fast that time. I figured that was because I'd said there was a baby involved. The officers weren't there too long. I knew Jane and my mom wouldn't let me see Emma, so I left; I had to work early the next day.

I hated not being able to see my niece, but I planned to come back after work.

The next day, I stalk the clock every second that passed. One tick of the minute hand seemed to last as long as three. Only fifteen more minutes until I was off work. My phone started ringing, and when I picked it up, I saw Mark's name flash across the screen. He normally never called me—he always texted me to call him so I knew this must be important. When I answered, he didn't say hi; he immediately told me that "they" had taken my niece. I could hear the sadness in his voice.

They? Who are they, and why did they take her?

I thought. I was silent. The only thing Mark could hear was my heavy breathing then replied with, "CPS." With worry in my voice I told him, "I'll be there as soon as possible!"

I grabbed my car keys then immediately clocked out of work. I didn't give a shit if my boss fired me for leaving early. It was an emergency.

I could barely hold back the tears as I dashed to my car. While I was speeding and weaving through traffic, all I cared about was getting to Mark's. It was irritating me that everyone was in the way, no one else seemed to have a sense of a rush, just like the day at the hospital. The only sound was the engine revving and my pitiful sobbing. A million thoughts raced through my mind. It was my fault. If I hadn't called the cops, she wouldn't have been taken by Child Protective Services, but if I hadn't intervened, she could have gotten hurt, or something worse could have happened.

"It's all your fault!" Those were the only words my mom said when I walked through the door. It wasn't all my fault, though. If she and Jane hadn't started fighting, or if Jane had let me take Emma to Mark's, then none of this would have happened.

My mind was spinning with visions of what must have happened. I could see Emma in her playpen while Jane was in the shower, and my mom was in the kitchen. A knock on the door. The two cops pushed through, holding my mom back, as the caseworker grabbed Emma from her playpen.

I didn't hear Emma's screams, but my head ached as if I did. I wondered where Mark was when they came for her. Maybe if he'd been there, he could have kept them from taking her.

The court ordered us to have a supervised visit with Emma twice a week, but it was a few weeks before we got to see her for the first time. Those were the hardest few weeks of my life. I was so depressed, but I kept a smile on my face for Emma. It was extremely hard, but I didn't want her to see my pain, and I didn't want to make her worry. Deep down, though, I was scared. I was scared that she was afraid and sad. I was terrified that she would hate me when she became old enough to understand what happened.

Mark and I were thrilled every time we got to see her, but my mom was always vexed. She talked way too much and would whisper things like, "Don't worry we" save you, you don't belong here with the people who stole you," to Emma as if we weren't being watched on video. The visits eventually were reduced to once a week and then every other week.

I started cutting myself. I would cut my thighs, my wrists, and even my ankles—anywhere that I could hide the cuts from where someone could see them. I felt so much pain, and I didn't know how *not* to feel it. I self-harmed as a distraction from what I was feeling inside. The first time I held the razor blade, my hands shook. I was lost and broken. With tears forming in my eyes, I started with a small slit on the edge of my left wrist. I was afraid to cut too deep. I didn't want to die; I just needed to feel pain other than what my heart was feeling. I watched the blood form at the incision. I just stared at it. I couldn't move my eyes away, like I was lost in a trance.

I cut a second time, running the corner of the blade a little deeper and longer across the inside of my forearm. The blood formed faster the second time. The cut was worse than I'd thought, so I switched to my right wrist. I became dicey and cut deeper, wider slits. I loved the distraction it caused, so I did it often when I was sad. Sometimes, I would do tiny knicks if I was in a hurry or had things to do that day. It became my addiction to watch my blood roll down my arms.

I couldn't let Emma see. The next time I visited her, I wore a long-sleeved shirt even though it was ninety degrees outside. When Mark or my mom asked me why

I was dressed that way, I would say I had chills. They never seemed interested in my well-being, though, and they never asked if I was okay, which caused me to cut even more. I was in so much pain emotionally that I wanted to take away from it, physically. No one ever found out I was cutting. I even kept it away from my best friend Marianna, as best I could. She most likely had seen the scabbed lines but never judged me.

Emma was placed in a foster home, and my mom wasn't okay with that. She stalked the foster parents on Facebook, followed them home from the store, and waited up the street to watch them come and go from their house. It was like she was on the show *Cheaters*, trying to catch her boyfriend being unfaithful. I remember once my mom rushed Mark and I to get into the car. "They're getting away, speed up!" I heard my mom yell to Mark. We followed in our car behind the vehicle of the foster family who had Emma in the back seat, through two towns before we lost them on a back road. Emma's foster family sent her back into the Foster Care system because of the harassment from my mom.

It was a hot summer day the afternoon when the second foster family had caught part of Emma's arm in the seat belt when they clicked her into her car seat.

The pain and heat caused her to have a seizure. The foster parents who had Emma in the second placement had enough of my mom terrorizing them, so they too returned Emma to the system.

Of course, I was terribly upset, but accidents happen. It wasn't like they were trying to cause her harm, but my parents didn't see it as an accident. As hard as it was, I would sometimes miss the scheduled time for a visit with Emma so that I didn't have to be around my mom. I didn't want the caseworker to think I was siding with her. Sometimes, I would wait until I saw Mark and my mom leave the building. Then I'd sneak around to the side door, hoping I could get a quick visit alone; it was a gamble worth taking. Usually, it worked, and I would spend thirty minutes with Emma. I shouldn't have let the fear that my mom and Mark would find out I was sneaking behind their backs impact me so much, but it did. I got paranoid that they were always watching me, like they did to almost everyone involved in our lives.

I kept a positive face every time I saw Emma because she didn't need to see the sadness. I needed to stay strong for her; she was too little to not have hope. Emma was placed in another home, but they too returned her within days because of my mom and her stalking antics. My mom accused them of wrongdoing to the caseworkers, like she had with the second family; the family chose to protect themselves from her lies. They didn't feel safe having Emma because they didn't know how far my mom would go. Before Emma was even two, she was in at least three different foster homes. The caseworker told my mom that she had to have her own supervised visits, separate from Mark, Jane, and me.

"Not unless Jane comes with me," my mom said and my sister didn't have the luxury of making a choice. The caseworker agreed because he wanted Emma and her mom to see each other.

My mom filed suit against Child Protective Services (CPS) because of corruption. She was known for filing random lawsuits, and for some reason, she thought they would help her. She had won only about three of her twenty previous lawsuits. She would say everyone was in "cahoots" with one another—the judge was being paid by the caseworker to judge in CPS's favor, according to her. She never once stopped to think about the damage she was causing, not only to Jane and Emma but to herself. My mom was like a wrecking ball, taking down anything and everyone in her path.

Every few weeks, we had to go to a court hearing. I always sat next to Mark, as far away from my mom as possible. Emma's dad, Joseph, was there every time with his dad. They always sat a couple of rows back. Shortly after the first couple of hearings, Joseph's aunt and her husband started coming, sitting next to his dad and him.

The judge called for my sister to come forward, but my mom approached the judge's stand in Jane's place.

"I'm Jane's guardian ad litem and her attorney for the case," my mom told the judge. To this day, I have not seen paperwork proving she was. She acted like a high-profile lawyer,—there's a saying that someone who represents himself in court has a fool for a client—my mom thought she could outsmart everyone else in the room. *Nonsense*, I thought, *No way in hell will my sister get custody of her child by having our mom represent her.*

I hated going to the hearings, but I never missed one. The judge wanted to grant reunification to my sister, but they required my mom to get a court-ordered mental health evaluation. She refused, and I was instantly confused as to why. She always told the court that she was stable, but she wouldn't take a mental test proving she was okay. Her refusal to take the test obviously raised eyebrows and looked bad to everyone on the outside. My mom never stopped fighting them though—she was tough—and she didn't stop reminding me that this was all my fault.

Joseph's aunt Ivy approached Jane one day before the court hearing to tell her that they loved her. My mom saw and moved to get between them in a heartbeat.

"Never speak to my daughter," she told Ivy. She muttered something else but I couldn't hear it.

My sister looked so lost. Mom still wouldn't let Joseph speak to Jane either.

When the judge called me to the stand, I could barely speak. He asked me to tell the court what had happened to cause Emma to go into the system that day and asked if I agreed with the reunification of Emma and Jane.

My voice didn't feel like my own as I spoke into the tiny microphone on the stand. I watched the court stenographer typing away quickly at the keyboard connected to the screen, then my eyes darted everywhere around the room. I needed to feel some kind of comfort that was not present in the courtroom. I blubbered to the judge, "I just want my niece to be happy, and I want to get to see her." I wanted so badly to tell him that I didn't agree with reunification if my mom was still in the picture, but I couldn't find the words; I knew if I said what I wanted, my mom would be livid when I went to her house. I could barely keep it together; I was a sobbing baby.

The judge could see how upset I was, so he let me leave the stand. My mom's eyes were like laser beams, piercing my skin as I passed her to get to my seat. My heart was ripped right down the middle. I was sad that I was wanting the ruling to go in favor of CPS; sad that I was letting my mom down, but I didn't agree with her.

At the final court hearing, guardianship was granted to Ivy and her husband. My mom was furious, of course, because she wasn't getting Emma. I wrote my name and contact information on a piece of paper and passed it to Ivy. I didn't give a shit if my mom saw; I didn't want to lose my niece. I sent Joseph a message, pleading with him to not take Emma away from me. I told him I had nothing to do with the situation; it was all my mom's doing.

He responded, saying it wasn't up to him. I was devastated. Half of my heart had been ripped from my chest. At that time, I didn't know that he wasn't stable enough to take care of Emma. I blamed my mom, but was it my fault too? At that point, I just wanted to crawl into a hole and die.

A few weeks passed—although it felt like months—when I got an email from Ivy. She was very standoffish, but I didn't blame her. In her eyes, I was my mom's child, so I was probably like her—except I wasn't. I wanted nothing more than to tell her that. I so badly wanted to explain everything that happened. I wanted to let her know that my relationship with my mom started failing when my niece was taken into CPS. It was falling between the cracks, and I didn't care to pick up the pieces. Sometimes, it seemed like it had been a long time coming, as if my life was destined to put that wedge between my mom and me.

Ivy agreed to supervised visits at the CPS office. She wanted Jane and me there but not my mom because once Ivy got guardianship of Emma, my mom started slandering Ivy's name on social media. My mom came with us anyway. We only got two visits before Ivy put a stop to them because my mom made a fool of herself.

I felt bad for Ivy because my mom was sending her threats and saying awful things about her online. I wouldn't want anything to do with someone like that either, but I hated that she was taking the visits away from me too. I had finally moved two spaces forward on the game board, then I was quickly pushed back and I was at the start line all over again. My mom was like Swiper from *Dora the Explorer* except she didn't listen when someone told her, "No swiping."

I sent Ivy a message almost every day to thank her for taking my niece; if she hadn't, I didn't know where Emma would have ended up. Two weeks later, Ivy responded. She said she would love for me to come out to their house alone, if she could get the okay from the caseworker. I was thrilled!

Emma had turned three and was growing super-fast. The drive to Ivy's house took me about thirty minutes. I was so nervous, driving down the winding roads and up the steep hills. I first saw a big red barn and then their house. I couldn't help but smile. Her home was beautiful with so much land. I was relieved that Emma would get to grow up in such a lovely place.

A tiny part of me was sad, though, because I wouldn't get to be there every step of the way. I walked in through the garage door, which led into a short hallway by the washer and dryer. Emma jumped into my arms, and I lost all control. I finally felt some relief, some happiness. I played every game she wanted to play and read to her. I was her pony when she wanted to be a cowgirl. We started having more visits like this, once Ivy got the official okay from the caseworker. It annoyed me that she had to go through the caseworker. I didn't understand, but I accepted it because that meant I would get to see Emma more.

Ivy's husband was still iffy about me and questioned me a lot because through his eyes, he saw my mom. I couldn't seem to prove to him that I was nothing like her. I just had to hope he could believe me, sooner rather than later. I was tired of having to prove myself to everyone.

As of this writing, things are *so much* better. Emma is still in my life, and I'm still in hers. I go to her cheer practices, dance recitals, gymnastics, and just about anything I'm able to be involved in. I even got to take her to her first day of preschool. We had a slumber party the night before and painted our nails after jumping on the trampoline for what felt like hours.

I used to think about dying because life got so hard, but now, I'm glad I didn't give up. My sweet little niece was one of the main reasons why I didn't give up. I need to show her I have strength so she knows she can overcome anything.

Emma,

What a blessing you are! Never doubt or question your worth. I never want you to feel the pain I felt; you're never going to be alone. I let the absence of my dad affect me more than it should have, and I don't want that to happen to you because of your mom. Your mother loves you, but she is lost right now. I know, deep down, she wants nothing more than to hold you. You must stay strong for her so that one day, she can maybe find her own strength. You make me so proud, and I know she is proud of you too, even though she can't tell you that herself. Always kiss your nana good night. Nana is your guardian angel. I'm so thankful we have her in our lives. Always be kind to others and tell those you care for that you love them.

You're going to do amazing things in this lifetime, and you're beyond loved. Don't ever forget that!

Love,

Your aunt,
E

CHAPTER FIVE

Long-lost
/ˈlôNG ˈ-lôst/

adjective
lost or absent for a long time

"Hanna is an awful human being, Elle." This was one of my mom's favorite things to say to me. My mom always spoke badly about her. She gave me reason after reason why I shouldn't have anything to do with Hanna—she was in gangs, did a lot of drugs, and hung around with all the wrong people. Hanna must have forgotten she was white because she only hung out with African Americans, and my mom hated that. I was young, so I believed every word she said.

When I was about fourteen years old, Hanna contacted me. I didn't want anything to do with this person whom my mom had spoken so badly about. She knew immediately that our mom had filled my head with bullshit from all the stories I repeated to her. I wanted to know Hanna, actually *know* her, so I stayed in contact with her for a while. After all, she was my long-lost sister.

When I got home from school, I always called "dibs" on the computer. I would chuck my backpack on the couch, toss my jacket wherever it was convenient, and run over to the old office chair. My body became one with that chair. If I was thirsty, I would push off the floor with my feet so the chair would roll into the kitchen. My mom limited me to only an hour on the computer, and I didn't want to waste any time talking to Hanna.

My mom noticed that I had stopped going outside and playing in the yard as much as I used to. She could see that my only concern was the "stupid computer." I became paranoid with my mom keeping track. I felt like I always needed to watch over my shoulder to see if my mom was keeping a close eye on my every move. That's something I often felt in my childhood—paranoia. I was afraid I would get into trouble for going behind my mom's back under her roof.

I told Hanna that I had a feeling our mom was

going to find out we were talking. My sister asked me for my address and told me she was sending me money to get a cheap phone, and she would send me Virgin Mobile top-up cards each month so we could keep talking. It was so scary, but it was also thrilling that I had something I could keep as my dirty little secret. I felt so rebellious.

I loved hearing about Hanna's awesome life. She had three kids (soon to be four), two bachelor's degrees, and was working nonstop. She was working for a low-privilege school a few towns away from where she lived as the culinary arts instructor. Her jobs were the coolest. Before she became a chef, she had a job inspecting bugs to identify how long someone had been dead.

Months went by before my mom found out I had a phone. She knew everything, but somehow, she didn't know about my secret. On the day she saw me on my phone, however, is when the world stopped.

I wasn't sure what to tell her. I imagined her saying *Why do you have a phone, and why did you keep it from me? You must be up to something.*

It was unfair that I felt like I was doing wrong by talking to my sister, so I lied and told her my boyfriend had bought me the phone. She didn't say anything for a few minutes. My ears rang from the dead silence and piercing look she gave me. *Please, please, please believe me.* I thought. I was pleading with God or whoever was above to make her believe my lie. My lungs felt like they were shrinking since I was holding my breath.

Finally, she asked "Why did he buy you a phone a phone?"

I shrugged. "So we can talk more." I slowly shut the door to my room because I was afraid that if I slammed it, she would catch on to my white lie. That's all it was—a little white lie—so why was I so afraid?

She fell for my bogus reason. I was so thankful, but it made her more curious and nosier about my every action. I constantly deleted my texts and recent call history, fearing she would go through my phone. When I went to school, I would slip my phone in my backpack pocket. If I needed to take a shit, then my phone came with me. I didn't set it down anywhere. My phone was my precious belonging, and it always had to be with me.

My mom was extremely annoyed. I had something of my own that she didn't get to control, and that got under her skin. My mom started checking my mail if I got any. I knew I was toast when I saw the mailman's truck pull up. Mentally, I kicked myself over and over, thinking of how stupid Hanna and I were to not have sent my mail to my friend's house.

The mailman hopped out of the small mail truck and walked up to our front door. Before he could place the mail in the mailbox, my mom snatched it from his hands and shut the door.

She went through each envelope, occasionally saying *mm-hm* or just slightly nodding. *Stick a fork in me,* I thought, *because I'm done for.* The last envelope she looked at was from Hanna, addressed to me. My mom ripped it open and saw the Virgin Mobile card. The blood drained from my face, and my heart started pounding. I wanted to run to my room, but my legs wouldn't move. It was like my brain was no longer connected to the rest of my body; like two pieces of concrete were across my feet.

"I can't believe you lied to me!" The words felt like needles stabbing me in the back of the neck. She grabbed my phone from my pocket and dialed Hanna. I skulked into the other room but could hear Mom yelling from the kitchen. I felt like I had committed a crime, but all I had done was keep in contact with my sister. There was nothing I could do. I felt so guilty about Hanna.

I was grounded indefinitely. I was only allowed to

go to school and I had to come straight home. When the neighborhood kids told me that they were all going to play baseball in someone's yard, I lied about why I couldn't join. My mom was so mad at me for lying to her, but now I had to lie to everyone else to keep her happy.

Being grounded didn't last long because Mark had a talk with my mom. He somehow managed to get her to loosen up on my strings. I did always think he was smooth, like butter, and I was so thankful I had him to play the referee. My mom gave me my phone back, as long as I promised to not lie to her again. Of course, I agreed.

My and Hanna's conversations stopped after Mom found out we had been talking. It didn't cross my mind much because I was so busy with school and choir. I got to play baseball with the neighbor kids, and I felt like I had somewhat of a social life again.

On the bus ride home, I came across my sister's and my texts. I almost missed my bus stop because I was in a reverie, re-reading our words. I needed to reach out to her to apologize, but I also didn't want to get into even more trouble with my mom. I was so tired of spending all my time making my mom happy and not taking care of my own happiness. The bus stopped moving, and I stepped down the stairs. Instead of going left toward my house, I went right so I could call Hanna. I went right because I was tired of always feeling wrong.

Hanna and I caught up. I told her about everything, including my boyfriend, my classes, and anything else I could think of. Hanna was so easy to talk to; I wished I knew her. I needed to know her. When I told her that I wanted to meet her, she said she would send me a Greyhound bus ticket to come see her in Illinois, but this time, she would send it to my friend's house in case our mom still checked my mail. I was so excited! This was going to be my first trip somewhere by myself; the only problem was figuring out what I was going to tell my mom.

My feet paced so much that the floor could have fallen beneath me. A few days later, I mustered up the courage to tell my mom but I made sure Mark was within reach. At first, I stood in front of her, not saying anything. All the courage I had vanished, like the coin up the magician's sleeve. My mom looked at me with annoyance because I wasn't saying anything, but luckily, Mark stepped in. He was much easier to talk to so when he asked me what I needed to say, it just flowed out of me.

My words were like a long run-on sentence; I couldn't slow down because I knew she would have so much to say, just from the look on her face. If I let her talk, she wouldn't stop to breathe. After my final word escaped my lips, I inhaled a deep breath and just looked at my mom and Mark. *Say something, anything!* said the tiny voice in my head.

My mom said nothing. Mark was the first person to speak "I think that is a great idea." Then he nudged my mom for her to say something.

"Fine." That's all she said before she pushed between Mark and me to enter the kitchen.

The summer break before my freshman year was approaching fast, and the day for me to get on the bus was right around the corner. My mom was the most nervous. She tried to talk me out of going, saying things like, "God is going to judge you for going against your mother's wishes," or "That bus is going to get into a wreck, explode, and you'll die," or "Maybe terrorists will take over the bus," but; I wouldn't change my mind. I was going, and that was final. She told me to call her every day, and I told her I would. I mostly agreed just to get her off my case.

The ride to Illinois was so much fun and didn't

seem to take as long as I'd expected. I made a few new friends on the ride, and that made time go by smoothly. I never got bored.

When I heard, "Attention passengers: our next stop is Illinois," thrilled was all I felt. I was about to meet my sister for the first time and see for myself how "awful" she really was. The bus squealed to a stop as we arrived. I stood up from my seat and grabbed my small backpack. I practically raced to the door before anyone else could get up. My shampoo slipped out of my bag and rolled on the floor but I didn't stop to pick it up. My eyes darted. I looked around at all the people in the station and finally stopped on her.

Hanna was the lady by the soda machine who started "ugly crying" when she saw me. She pulled the guy's shirt next to her, saying, "Look! There's my sister; that's her!"

I wasn't sure what to do. I was very awkward back then. I didn't hug much, but she grabbed me and wrapped her arms around me so tight. I lifted my arms around her shoulders and held on to her too. Her sobbing got heavier, and I started to ugly cry with her. This big, tall, dark man standing with two short ladies, both crying, was probably humorous for everyone in

the bus station. This woman didn't look like the monster my mom had always described.

One of the first things we did was go by the bank
so she could get some money for our upcoming she-
nanigans. When we got to her house, her kids were
excited to meet me, and I was excited to meet them.
I felt like it wasn't my first time standing in her big
living room. Hanna, my niece Diamond, and I went
to the mall and then the art museum on my second
day. I got my first tattoo with Hanna. She was going
to her tattoo artist for a Friday-the-thirteenth tattoo. She had so many tattoos. I had sworn I never
wanted one, but I quickly changed my mind. The
small Friday-the-thirteenth star I had picked out became very large and covered my whole hip. Her tattoo
artist didn't add the number thirteen to my array of
stars; I assume he didn't because the numbers would
have looked odd.

I even let Hanna put hot pink and platinum blonde
in my hair, even though a week before, I had disliked
pink. I felt like she brought out another side of me I
hadn't known existed.

This sister of mine didn't suck at all. She was about
fifteen years older than me, but she was the coolest.
She didn't act like the usual, boring thirty-year-old's

I was used to meeting. Even with all those years we didn't spend together, we got along so well. We made similar stupid jokes that we thought were hilarious, and we both were weirdos. I couldn't believe our mother had kept us apart, just because Hanna didn't talk to Mom.

She told me something that you'd think could only happen in a movie. When Hanna was about ten years old, it was just her and our mom living together in a small apartment. Hanna's dad and my mom were divorced, but Mom was still very hostile about it. Even to this day, I believe she is still angry about it. Hanna walked into the kitchen to get juice or food. My mom grabbed a knife and started screaming at the top of her lungs that she was going to kill herself, while stabbing around her fingers like that weird game drunk people play.

Of course, my sister freaked out and took off running out of the front door. She ran down the street to the college to get help. Two students came back to the house with her, but by then, our mom was doing the dishes. My mom laughed and asked why Hanna had run off—she acted as if nothing had happened and Hanna was just being dramatic. When Hanna told me this story, I imagined those creepy robot women that are like housewives. *Hello, honey, how was your day?* As if they are always happy and nothing could go wrong.

That's what my mom reminds me of. Nothing can possibly go wrong in her mind. She's very sly and manipulative at making it seem that way. When Hanna was young, before Jane and I were born, our mom would send Hanna to live with her dad. Then she would call him and accuse him of kidnapping Hanna and plead for him to give her back. Shortly after she'd get Hanna back, she'd send her back to him. It was an endless cycle. It fucked up Hanna's relationship with her dad for a long time.

She ended up "adopting" another woman as her mom because she needed to fill the void that her biological mother had created. This woman adored Hanna and loved her so much. She taught her ways to not be like our mom. Hanna filled the gaps with people who loved and cherished her. They were the glue to fill the empty spots, and they stuck with her. I am so proud of my sister, and I really envy her for being so strong.

I'd much rather be like her than anything like our mom.

Hanna,

There are so many things I want to tell you, but I can't find all the words. I'm so lucky that I have you in my life. You were one of the only normal family members I had. If I hadn't had you to help me, I don't know where I would be today. Maybe I would have ended up like Mom. That still crosses my mind sometimes, and I have the fear that may happen one day. I will do everything I can to not let that happen. I'm so proud of you. You stayed strong, so when I needed it, I could be strong too. I look up to you so much. I wish we could have spent more time together when I was growing up. Things could have been so different. I'm so glad I have you now, though. You were the crutch to hold me up when I couldn't stand on my own. Thank you for everything you've ever done for me. It helped me more than you probably think. I love you so much!

Love,
Your little "seester", Elle

---

CHAPTER SIX

ex·em·plar
/igˈzemplär/

noun
a person or thing serving as a typical example or excellent model

My mom met Mark when I was about six months old. She was around thirty-eight years old, so he was about twenty-four. He worked at a tire shop with the name Mark in it. Mom had gone there because she needed new tires before getting out of town. "People" were after her; I can only guess from stories that the "people" were Hanna's dad and stepmom along with my biological father.

One of her rear doors was barely hanging on to the car when she pulled in. Mark saw Jane, about four years old, and a baby in a car seat in the back. He and my mom had small talk after he introduced himself. When he said his name was Mark, she probably internally screamed because she thought he owned the company; he must have been *the* Mark of the shop. I would bet money that is one of the biggest reasons she wanted him around—only because she thought he was filthy rich.

Mark never told me much about their relationship, so I can only describe my own experiences around them. The two of them never got married, and I recall them kissing or holding hands only a few times when I was younger than eight. They showed little to no affection to each other in front of Jane and me. When people would ask me how Mark was related to me, I would tell them he was my stepdad, but technically, he was a man who was in a relationship with my mom and had stayed around to take care of my sister and me.

Not a lot of people knew they were never married so I always thought, *What's the point?* It was too complicated to explain every single time someone asked.

She brainwashed and manipulated him a lot. One example: he asked me why I spent ten dollars on a meal because that was too much money; if we as a family ever ate out, we could only get food from the dollar menu. I knew money was always a struggle—ever since I was a kid—and I felt it really affected him because my mom was so bad with her finances. He has said he stayed for me, but I think it's also because he feels bad for my mom. Maybe the love he has for her gets in the way of his rational thinking. It may have eaten away at his conscience forever if he had left.

Even though she was cruel to him, he still reached out a helping hand to her anytime she needed it but she never truly appreciated it. She never appreciated him. Mark put her above himself and always chose to help her instead of leaving town and doing something for himself. His family never really liked my mom. They could see something in her that he couldn't, maybe he saw it too but turned his head the other way. It's like he picked her over them.

These days, his health isn't too great, and all I wish for him is that he will do everything he has ever wanted to do before it's too late. My mom has taken so much from him, including his happiness, but she can never put a wedge between him and me. I'm so thankful he sacrificed and put up with her illness because without him, I don't know where I would be today.

He was my best friend. Pictures from my life are rare, but one of my favorites is of him and me, looking through the mail together. I was about three years old. We looked so happy, and it hurts me that I can't say that I knew I was happy back then.

When I was younger, I used to get so mad at Mark because he was overprotective. I tried to keep a wall between him and any friends I had because he seemed scary. Everyone loved him when they got to know him, though. Mark made the lamest jokes that no one else would get or think were funny; they were bad dad jokes. Some would call it dry humor. They just didn't get him like I did.

He was my modern-day cab driver for my friends and me when I was a kid. He would say something and keep a stern face, and everyone would think he was angry. Then I would follow up with a sarcastic joke, and they would look at me like I was out of my mind because they thought he was actually upset, yet I always laughed. Mark would then shoot me a playful smirk. I tried to explain to my friends that if he was angry, they would know.

That's one of the many things I adopted from him. I was super-easygoing, but if you did something to upset me, you'd know instantly. Mark is like King Kong—the mighty, powerful protector who can cause destruction but with a huge heart of gold. He is one of the kindest people I know, and that's why I can't wrap my head around why he stuck around my mom for so long.

I'm sorely disappointed that I can't remember anything good from my childhood because he always spoke of how much fun we had.

Mark,

If you're reading this, I want you to know I love you, and you mean so much to me. I know we have had our ups and downs, but you never left. You never gave up on me. My mom has pushed so many good things away from me, but she never pushed you out. I'm sorry if I have ever taken you for granted. You have been a guardian angel to me. I wish that my mom had let you adopt me. Thanks for being the dad I never had and for creating memories for us.

You have been the best dad in this world. I try to smile when I'm sad because I think about the happiness it brought to you. I don't remember the good and fun things we did because Mom covered them with her negativity, but I'm so happy you will always have those memories. I'm sorry I don't remember everything we did, but what I do remember are some of the best memories I have. I will keep them for the rest of my life. You deserve to be happy because you did everything you could to make me happy. You always made me laugh and made sure I wasn't hungry. You always cared for me. You are a blessing, and I am so grateful. Thank you!

Love,
Your daughter Elle

---

CHAPTER SEVEN

nar·cis·sist

/ˈnärsəsəst/

noun
a person who has an excessive interest in
or admiration of themselves

Loving and beautiful is how I would describe my
mother Lauren; a beautiful disaster. When I was little,
she kept every drawing and card that I made for her.
She always told me how much she loved them and how
much she adored me.

Mark, Jane, Mom, and I always had family outings
when I was very young. We took tons of pictures together and went to a local theme park—Kiddie Land—
almost every weekend. Jane and I fought over having
Mom's attention, which I'd always had because I was

the baby. It was like I was attached to my mom's hip. Every night, I slept in Mom's bed with her. My sister was extremely jealous and was extra mean to me because of it.

When I was younger, I hated that my mom didn't allow me to do anything, and I was envious that Jane could do whatever she wanted. I wasn't allowed to go to my friends' houses unless my mom had their parents' phone number and had met them. Any parent would want contact information in case of an emergency, but it was different situation for me. My mom was overly cautious; so, upon her meeting parents, I always feared that they would tell their child that we couldn't be friends anymore.

I could agree that my mom's parenting was a bit much, such as the time she dropped me off at a birthday party. I had been there for about fifteen minutes playing in the backyard, when one of the kids asked, "Is your mom coming in?" Utterly confused, I glanced over by the fence and saw her little red car. We made immediate eye contact and I was horrified to know she never left. She just sat in her car watching me.

The older I got, the more embarrassed I became of her. My birthday parties became her birthday parties. Somehow, she was able to take all the attention from me and put it on herself. She made sure that the world revolved around her, and she was living her life through me. Every year, fewer and fewer kids would come to my birthday party. The last party I had at my house was when I was ten, and only two girls showed up. I wasn't even friends with one girl, but her mom knew my mom. I'm sure that's why she came.

The other girl left before the party even started, so I was stuck celebrating "my mom's" birthday party with a girl who didn't even like me. At the party, we bobbed for apples, and the girl won the dollar at the bottom of one of the apples. My mom made me feel lousy for not winning; that's why I'm so competitive now. Sometimes, I wish I wasn't competitive because I wouldn't feel the need to be the best. I like to win so I can get praise; that was something I didn't get when during my childhood.

After that party, I decided I no longer wanted people to come over to celebrate my birthday. My mom didn't understand why because, of course, she thought the parties were fun.

I had my first "boyfriend" in elementary school. His name was Robby, and he was my best friend. He had curly red hair and the cutest freckles. My mom was friends with his mom, so I was allowed to go to go to Robby's house but only when his mom was home. I was there after school every day and on the weekends. We jumped on the trampoline, played hide-and-seek, or competed for first place with a video game. I tried to go there so Robby didn't have to come to my house. My mom complained and told me that if I wanted to go to his house, then we had to play at ours sometimes too.

It was cool the first few times. We played Mario World on Nintendo with Mark, and we had a lot of fun. It annoyed my mom that she wasn't part of the games we played. I don't know what got into her head, but she looked right at Robby and told him we were related. She called us "kissing cousins," and then she pulled out the genealogy scroll and explained how we came from royalty.

For my being a princess, I sure didn't look like one, nor did we have the money royalty had. My mom would give me bowl cuts and not care how I was dressed. My outfit usually consisted of a dingy white T-shirt and windbreaker pants.

One of the saddest memories I have is from third grade. I must have been late for the bus, or maybe my mom was in a hurry to drop me off at school but she sent me to class with tangled, unbrushed hair. As I sat down in my seat, a boy I thought was cute commented,

"You couldn't even brush your hair today?" Back then I would cry at the drop of a dime, so that's what I did. I lay my head down on the desk and softly cried, with my arms wrapped around my face. I tried to be quiet so no one else would notice but they all did.

Mrs. Jones was my teacher that year. She was from Texas and was the sweetest teacher I had. She always passed out sour-straw candies to us when we did well on tests. She was tall, with short, curly brown hair, and her breath always reeked of coffee. Mrs. Jones was in her office, pouring herself a cup of coffee when another kid made a comment about my gross hair. Other students burst into laughter, and I cried even harder. Mrs. Jones appeared in the doorway and hollered, "What is going on in here?" Everyone sat up straight in their seats and got quiet, except for a few snickers coming from different corners of the room.

Mrs. Jones approached my desk and knelt next to me. "Oh, sweetie, what's the matter?"

I sniffled as I pointed up to my hair. She stood up quickly and told the class that if they stayed quiet while we went to her office, she would give out some sour straws. Everyone kept their mouths shut, but when I walked past them, holding her hand, they quietly giggled.

"Did you get sent to school today with your hair all tangly?" she asked.

"Mm-hm," I mumbled.

"Well, don't you worry, sweetheart. I will fix this for you." She ushered me to her rolling office chair. She had a spray bottle in her right hand and a big comb in her left. I was so sad and embarrassed as she spritzed water on my matted, nest of hair.

"I'm sorry. I'm such a loser." I looked at her through my tear-filled eyes.

"Oh, no honey! Don't you ever say that about yourself. You're beautiful, and you need to always keep a smile on that pretty face of yours!" she cooed as she brushed out the last tangle in my hair then she placed a bobby pin to pull my bangs from my eyes.

I returned to my desk, and Mrs. Jones brought out the sour straws for everyone. When she got to my desk, she gave me three and winked at me.

People started spreading the rumor that I was royalty around the school. When kids would point at me, I imagined them saying, "What kind of princess has messy hair and dresses like that?" Everyone made fun of me, and then Robby stopped talking to me. I was devastated. I knew we couldn't be related just because he had red hair and supposedly my royal family in Ireland did too. I didn't even like the idea of being a princess, but my mom told everyone that I was. I didn't believe it. I had never heard of the so-called family on the scroll she had. It looked like a photo-shopped paper that had been weathered to make it appear old.

I completely stopped bringing anyone over because she would bring out the scroll. It was so uncomfortable, and I kept apologizing to my friends. They would walk out the door, leaving the weirdo (me) with the kooky mom to go hang out with their cool friends. I felt like such a misfit.

That was the start of my shitty life. Kids were mean to me, without a doubt. They would purposely trip me in the hall, throw things at me, and call me names. One student even pulled my pants down in gym class in front of everyone. When that pulled down my pants. I froze, and all the other kids stopped in their tracks to look at me. The boy who did it pointed and laughed at me. The PE teacher yelled at everyone to continue what they were doing and then pulled me to the side. I explained what had happened, but it was like the teacher didn't believe me. I cried when I lied and said I needed to use the restroom. I walked quickly away from everyone and waited in the restroom until lunch period. I couldn't trust anyone, not even adults. I had a fear of walking alone in the halls.

When I was in my early teens, I sometimes had friends over to hang out. My mom would steal the show like she had done when I was younger. She would do silly dances and tell the stories about me that I hated the most and, of course, she'd roll out the scroll. I felt ten all over again. I couldn't seem to get out of her clutches. When my friends and I went to my room to watch TV, Mom came too. She seemed to think she was our age and wanted to feel included.

The rumors of my crazy family followed me wherever I went. When I came home crying because kids had hurt me, Mom would tell me she was going to sue those kids' parents. I was living in hell. When I cried, I just wanted to be comforted by my mom; instead, she threatened everyone. Eventually, I tried to hide when I was sad.

I bottled everything up inside, and I felt horrible for lying to my mom when I was sad, but it just felt easier to keep it from her. *'I'm fine; everything's fine,'* I would say to myself when I stepped off the bus to head home. The threats of lawsuits added to the name-calling and the rumors. If a kid started picking on me, another kid would say, "You better stop doing that unless you want to get sued." It was like a bowl of pepper, and I was the toothpick. Put me in the middle, and everyone scattered, just as the pepper did.

I spent lunch period sitting alone most of the time. I ate my lunch in the hall by the water fountain or in the bathroom with the stall door locked and my backpack pressed against it.

In middle school, I stopped having friends over. I went to their houses more to keep them away from my mom. People started liking me again.

My mom was the epitome of a helicopter mom. By the time I was almost fifteen, I still wasn't allowed to go to the mall with the other kids, so I'd just say that I was too busy to go. Others started the not-so-awful rumor that I was rich, and that's why I wouldn't hang out with them. I wish that one had been true.

I made a lot of excuses so that people wouldn't make fun of me anymore. I lost one of my best friends because my mom accused her of stealing my phone. My friend Sara and I were out in the snow, and I dropped my phone as we were running and laughing. She never took my phone, but Mom didn't believe that I had dropped it no matter how many times I explained what happened. Sara and I walked every square foot of the parking lot we were in but never found it; that is why my mom said she had taken it. She called Sara's mom and threatened to sue them for my phone. Sara stopped talking to me.

I'd thought things had gotten better now that I was older, but after the phone incident, it all got bad again. I think Sara told people what had happened (I never asked her if she did, I just assumed she had) and I was made out to be a loser again. As much as I couldn't stand my mom, sometimes I couldn't stay mad at her. She was my mom, and I thought she cared; as if she did these things out of good intentions. She had brought me into the world, and, in my eyes, she was imperfectly perfect. She always bragged about being perfect, so it just stuck in my head.

I didn't have anyone else in my life besides my mom and Mark. Jane was the bad kid, and my mom always preached to me about what was right and wrong. She told me God would judge me soon because the end of days was right around the corner. I obeyed my mom because she put the fear of God in me. The end of days was "near" for about four different years. She had a date that God had given her when he came to her bedside, and that was when he was coming to make a judgment on everyone.

I was nervous and afraid that the world was ending.

I did everything I could to make sure I did the right thing, even when it seemed easier to do wrong. I lived in fear. I didn't want to go to hell, like my mom said I would, but Jane still did wrong. Freshman year if high school was when I started realizing that my mom may have a mental illness. Growing up, her behavior seemed to be normal to me until I started going over to different friend's houses and watching their families interact. The world didn't end. I was still breathing, and the world was still spinning. God never came.

Going to the doctor was always such a dreadful experience. I was never able to go by myself or speak to anyone. We would get taken back to a room and my mom would prep me for what she was going to tell them. She was good at mumbling snarky comments under her breath when the doctor and nurses spoke. The nurse would come in to ask me questions, but I would never get to respond because my mom would start bragging that she was a paramedic, a nurse's aide, and a lawyer. I could tell the nurse was getting frustrated, but she would try not to roll her eyes while my mom told her that she was one class away from a doctorate.

Once the doctor would write me a prescription, she would tell me, "We're not going to fill this. I'm not spending money on medication that I already have." At home she would pull out a big red plastic storage tub of antibiotics, which were either expired or weren't mine. I would swallow back the pills because I had no other choice. Half the time I didn't even know what I had taken.

My mom constantly was on the computer once my hour computer time was up, either reading medical news or organizing her next best coalition. She would tell her "followers" that she owned a battered women's shelter and a private investigation firm. It was shocking to me that she would pretend to try and give others hope that she could actually help them. She went as far as to ask for money from them and that money ended up getting spent on materialistic items for herself.

My mom used to send me links to join her family tree online. I got curious one day, so I looked at it. There were statements about all the careers she had achieved in her life, her royal family and she was working on writing another book; it was already lined up to be published. I knew that wasn't true because I was her kid. I never saw legitimate papers for any of her claims, and frankly, I knew it wasn't true because we weren't even one bit wealthy. We barely had money to pay the utilities and rent.

I had to share a room with my mom. My bed was in the opposite corner from hers. Instead of having a mattress and bed frame, I had a makeshift bed frame made out of storage tubs with an air mattress thrown on top; sometimes I wouldn't even be lucky enough to have the storage tubs so my air mattress was on the floor.

It seemed like almost every month; we would get a disconnection notice from the utility company. My mom took food from buffets and wrapped dinner rolls in napkins to shove in her purse to take home. She'd say it wasn't stealing since she had paid for the buffet. I was always embarrassed.

She made an entirely different persona for herself—of someone she wasn't. She never quite lived in the same realm as the rest of us. She seemed to adapt to other people's lives and make others believe it was her life too. I later found out from Hanna that it was her father who had Irish royalty in his family line, not our mom. My mom had created the scroll and gave herself a family name that wasn't even real that I know of. My mom never had proof of these claims.

One night my mom wanted me to watch the 1991 film, JFK. While watching, she pointed to a man and claimed that the actor was her father. I gave her a puzzled look because this man was not significant in the movie. She went on to tell me her father was killed in a premeditated plane crash by the government due to him knowing secret information about JFK's murder.

I found that very hard to believe. I'm sure it was a freak accident and the plane he was flying was old and faulty.

She always told me that her mom was killed intentionally through shock therapy; in reality, her mom overdosed on psychological medications and had a heart attack according to my mom's sister. I could never find death records of my grandparents' death and I don't even know their full names. I can't understand why my mom would tell things like this. Was she embarrassed that her life wasn't actually this exciting, or did she believe it all?

She took pride in doing amazing things in her life; she put on a good act. When it came to her knowledge of the law, I believed it all. I was in a car accident that I wasn't at fault for when I was a teenager, and I had no idea how to handle it or what I needed to do. I asked my mom for help; parents, especially moms, are supposed to be there for that sort of stuff. I found out though, that asking for her help was a mistake.

She typed up a paper for me to sign that stated once I received a settlement from the insurance company, I was to pay her ten percent above the cost of medical bills for the help I'd received from her. I didn't understand why she didn't just help me without any strings attached.

People paid her to assist them with their lawsuits because they believed she could really help them legally. She was so good with her words that it was hard not to believe her. She always sounded like she knew what she was talking about. She was good at making people believe her lies, and even I believed them.

When I was little, she would try to cause our car to be in the middle of accidents so she could get something out of it. It didn't matter if I was in the car; she just wanted to make a profit from everything. She was always a con artist.

My mom always talked about the people who had done her wrong in the past including the four men who had ruined her life. The first was my biological father, for lying about his age when they got married and then getting discharged from the military, kidnapping Jane, and because she had to sleep with him again to get Jane back.

The second was Hanna's dad, for cheating on Mom

with his now-wife, Cheri, when Mom and he were married. (In fact, he and my mom were already separated when that occurred and had filed for divorce.) My mom was just angry that he had found someone else and was moving on from her. All I ever heard was how conniving and evil Cheri was, how she stalked my mom and told lies about her; actually, it was the other way around. My mom posted awful comments on Facebook and stalked Cheri. I wouldn't be surprised if there were things like that on all her social media accounts. She has at least ten Twitter accounts with similar names and multiple Facebook accounts. She keeps tabs on others by hiding behind the screen. She said Cheri wanted to have her killed, just like the rest of the world did.

Then there was Sam, the guy who she caught going down on another guy at a party. I'm not sure why he is on the list of guys who ruined her life, but he is. I understand how that would break her heart, but they weren't married, and they were young. It's one of those things that should have been left in the past.

Last but not least is Mark; she faulted him for anything and everything else. She never talked about the good things he had done for her or the family, just the things she didn't like. I hated that she talked so badly about these men, but I especially hated how she talked about Mark. Even right in front of him, she would say awful things about him, comparing him to Hanna's dad.

Throughout my life, my mom has reminded me of everything she has done for me. If I ever borrowed money from her, she made me feel like shit by saying I wouldn't pay her back, or it'll take me forever to pay her back. It caused me not to want to ever to ask her for a dime. She would tell me how I owed her the world because she brought me into it and that I wouldn't be here if it weren't for her. Frankly, I would rather have not been brought into the world anyway. One minute, she told me how important I was; then, without saying the exact words, she let me know I was a mistake. That can fuck someone up, and it has messed with my head. I couldn't even go to her house within the last five years to visit without her freaking out. I got no time alone just to sit and talk or hang out with my sister.

One day when I when I was at my mom's house, she rudely said, "You'd better not be taking pictures of the inside of my house" —as if threatening me. She had too much crap, and she knew it. The last time I was in her house, her bedroom looked like it had when I lived with her. All the "projects" she was working on were scattered around the floor. My old "bed" —an air mattress on storage tubs—was still there and she had to maneuver around it all to get to her bed.

She thinks that the CIA and FBI tap her phone and hide in her air vents so I'm sure she thought I would send pictures to them or that I'm was giving my information to Hanna's stepmom to use against her. I know the CIA and FBI have better things to do. They don't even know her name, but she thinks they do. She believes all the nonsense she comes up with. It's hard not having my mother in my life—that is the hardest thing for anyone to go through. I wouldn't wish that on my worst enemy. Mom is just a text away, yet it's like she's in another galaxy.

My mom will never admit that something isn't right with her and that she needs help, but it's time I put the past behind me. I have left it there and have started a new chapter.

Dear Mom,

Do you ever think about how you got to where you are? Why did you let yourself get here? I wish you would have reached out for help. There's nothing wrong with that because everyone needs help sometimes. I wish that you would swallow your pride. You know something isn't right. I'm at the age now where I've realized I need to let go. I need to let go of this and what we could have been. I only have a few of positive memories; I only want to remember the good ones. I don't recall many good ones though. You have put such a sour taste in my mouth that I have always pushed people away because of it. When I have something good, but it isn't enough; there's always something better.

    I have let so many good things slip through my fingers, and I don't know why I'm like that. I only hurt myself when I imagine having you as my mom because that can never happen, not realistically. Not now. Not ever. I miss our having a mother-daughter day. You'd take me on a mini-shopping trip, and then you'd let me pick where we ate. That's one of my favorite memories. One of my favorite good memories I have, is when you would say "Elle, go outside and get the best-looking snow so we can make some ice cream." We used to watch movies together, and you were always the loudest fan, cheering for me at my volleyball games. You used to be proud of me, I thought. What happened?

I even miss your awful, embarrassing dance moves. You'd always do them in front of my friends, and I hated it, but I miss it now. I miss it so much. I miss it because it showed me you could let loose and have fun. It showed me that you were there in the moment and nowhere else. You're not capable of seeing what you did or taking the blame for any time you were wrong. Instead, you blamed me. You blamed Mark. You blamed Jane. You blamed everyone but yourself. I bottled everything up when I should have been able to talk to my mom, but your focus was elsewhere. It caused me to be aggressive. All I ever wanted was to come to you for anything. I was always angry. Do you know how many relationships I ruined because of you? I ruined myself because of you.

My sweetness and the naive part of me vanished when you vanished emotionally. I wish I would have stopped taking the blame. I always accepted it because I believed it. I should have stopped feeling guilty a long time ago, but you manipulated your way every time. When I decided I was done, you made me think I hurt your feelings. I didn't, though, did I? You only said I was hurting my mom so you could rope me back in and make me want to take care of you. You used the fact that you were my mom for all the wrong reasons. It was always my fault. At least, that's what I thought. It was my fault that you were so unhappy. I could have helped you, but I just didn't know how. I still don't. I'm not sorry anymore. You never were sorry for anything you did. You were perfect, at least you said that God told you that you were. You did no wrong.

I'm grieving over someone who is still here. Yet it feels like you're gone. I can almost reach out and touch you, but I don't know if you'd get angry. I text you to say happy birthday or happy Mother's Day, but I get nothing in return. Not even a simple thank you. The only time you text me is to bitch. You wonder why I stopped trying... well, that's why. You told me I was taking away your happiness no matter how hard I tried to make you smile. Excuses—you always made excuses, but you flipped the table and pointed your fingers at me. I have hurt myself physically, but you have never noticed because you don't seem to care. I never felt comfortable enough to tell you I have issues with my kidney and that I was hospitalized for a week because of it; I could have been placed on a ventilator.

I want to tell you about my day, about my jobs, about my relationship and about my cats and the silly things they do, but you don't listen if it isn't about you. I've tried. I've tried so hard, but you've shot me down so much that I don't even want to try anymore. I really want to hate you, Mom, but I can't. I can't hate you for the illness, but I can hate that you never got help. You never wanted to make things better. You said I was breaking your heart, but you've broken mine. The best thing I can do for myself is to move on, to try to be happy and think of myself for once.

I'm so happy I got away from your crazy. I think that is why you can't just love me for me because I chose not to be you. I'm happy with my life and where it is. I'm just sad that you aren't part of it. I just want, need, this hurt to go away—the hurt a mother takes away from her baby—but you were the one who put it there. I can't wait anymore for you to take it away because you didn't then, and you won't now.

I'll always remember you and cherish the good times we had. I miss you so much, but I must let go. I do want to thank you for writing those bad fairy tales on the small computer when I was a kid because you let me type some and even title yours. You showed me how to tell a story.

I'll always love you.

Love,
your daughter

---

na·ive

/nīˈēv/

adjective
a person or action showing a lack of experience, wisdom, or judgment

Everyone hopes for a perfect life—unlimited happiness, love, and a family to always be there whenever you need them. That's what I hoped for, but unfortunately, that wasn't the hand I was dealt. Instead, I folded my hand before I had the chance play it.

When I was little, I had so many hopes and dreams. I dreamed of a big wedding, becoming a famous singer, and having a family of my own. I never knew how hard any of that was to accomplish. My mom always told me that I was prettier and better than everyone else, and

I believed her. What a rude awakening I got. Growing up, I finally realized that every mom told her child that, and some of those children took it to heart. I didn't want to be like them. Even though I knew I was pretty, I didn't want others to think I was better than anyone else. I was kind to everyone, and that took a wrong turn.

I found out the hard way that other people didn't think as I did. If they were pretty or slightly smarter than others, they showed it. I got mistreated because I was too nice, too naive. People walked all over me as if I was their personal doormat. They took advantage of me, but I allowed it to happen because I thought they were my friends; I wanted them to be my friends. I had such a thin shell. Anytime someone was mean, my shell cracked a bit. I cried over anything. That just caused more name-calling, which in turn caused more tears to fall.

I wasn't special to anyone besides my mom and Mark. Jane was always doing bad things, and I swore I wouldn't do any of the things she did. I wanted to be better than she was, so I was always a good kid. I followed the rules.

We moved a lot, and I switched schools quite often. I hated it, but it helped my shell get thicker. I would make a new friend, and I'd think that friend-ship would last forever—a child's hope—but then my family would move so fast that I didn't even have a chance to tell that friend goodbye. I stopped opening up to people, and I became shallow. I thought there was no point in being the real me because I knew I wouldn't be around that long.

I mostly kept to myself. I was around four years old when we moved from Illinois to Oklahoma. Mark came along with us because he and my mom were practically married, at least, that's what I thought. My mom said that we moved because of Jane's dad. He wanted to kill Mom and take Jane again, so we left. We were on the run. It felt like we always were running, and that caused more fighting between my mom and Mark.

Off and on, he would move out and live in his own place. I was lonely because the family outings had slowed down, and I always had to play alone because Jane wouldn't play with me. I would create my own cooking show and pretend I was on TV. I made up everything in my head and played it out in our front yard. I had a good imagination; that's all I had.

We stayed in Miami, Oklahoma, for only a few months. I had trouble remembering anything because it was gone almost as quickly as it had appeared. We moved again to a small town called Norman, Oklahoma—a little tourist town where the locals were rich assholes and all the kids were the same as their parents. All of them were mean to anyone who wasn't well off like they were. The three months we spent there were the absolute worst. I don't remember much about that place, other than going to a school with the snobby kids and living in the basement of someone's house.

My mom knew the lady who owned the house, and she let us stay there for a little bit. She had a few kids that I would play with, but if Jane was around, they would purposely ignore me because Jane was the older, cooler one. I didn't let it bother me, at least not show that it bothered me. I had my own cooking show called "Cooking with Elle," and a different celebrity would be my co-host each time. I thought those kids were way too lame to be involved with a celebrity chef anyway.

I was always pretending I was someone I wasn't. I was in an International Scooter Championship race and took first place—okay, not really, but I rode my Razor scooter down that hill as fast as could. I imagined getting rushed by hundreds of fans who raised me on their shoulders and celebrated my victory.

"What are we cooking today?" my guest would ask.

"Today, I will show you all how to make my family recipe of lasagna." I would say. I would imagine my guest tasting a bite of my delicious lasagna and her eyes getting wide. Then she would tell the audience that they were all getting my cookbook, and the audience would lose their minds with excitement. There wasn't anything that I couldn't do. My résumé would have been the length of a dictionary.

Every day, I got up at 5:00 a.m. to lie on the couch with my mom and watch the local news on TV. *"Boy, what an exciting life I have"*, I thought sarcastically.

One day, Mark got a call from his sister, saying that we should move to Broken Arrow. It wasn't too far from where we were currently living, and we would be closer to his family. Mark's mom was getting older and needed checking on more. However, my mom wasn't thrilled about it because Mark's attention would be more focused on his family and not her. Within the next few weeks, however, we packed up what little stuff we had and made the short move. The small building down the road was where my new home would be for school. My routine was to keep to myself again because there was no telling how long I'd be there.

Months passed by and, amazingly, we were still there. I let my guard down for a little bit and ended up making a few friends. I had my "first kiss" during class naptime. A dorky boy was on a red-and-blue mat right next to mine. He kept trying to get my attention whenever I tried to fall asleep. He was the first friend I made in class. I rolled a little ball to him, and he rolled it back. We were young so we didn't realize there were rules against not sleeping. Other students were sleeping around us, and the teacher hadn't noticed that we were still awake. The ball rolled a bit too hard, and it almost bounced into the back of a little girl's head. She barely noticed, and the ball rolled to the middle of the floor.

I started to giggle and then he giggled, which caused me to get louder.

The teacher finally noticed and yelled at us. "This is your first and last warning, you two! Elle, you go over there!" She scolded at us while pointing that I should go the opposite direction of him. That didn't stop us. The boy crawled over to my mat, and that's when he laid a slobbery kiss on my lips. I was shocked. The teacher glanced over and spotted us. By the horrified look on her face, I knew she was furious. I was put out in the hall while our parents were called. I don't remember what my mom said or how Mark reacted; all I remember is being taken out of school.

I have a photograph of me painting a papier-mâché dinosaur in a gymnasium, but I have no recollection of where or when that was. There are hardly any pictures of me as a kid that I've seen. It makes me feel like I was never fully living my life—or at least I don't have memories of living it. Mark has claimed, though, that our family always had fun.

I remember a car wreck I got into with my mom and Jane. The other driver thought she could speed across the road to a parking lot, but she was wrong. She smashed into our van. I was put on a stretcher and taken into the hospital. We got a settlement around five thousand dollars, I think. My mom gave Jane and me one hundred dollars each—and blew the rest on herself.

As a family, we would go shopping. Mark and my mom would take us to the local theme park, but I have no memory of that, other than the picture of me as a toddler, sitting next to Mark on one of those kiddy roller coasters. He makes me feel like it's my fault for not remembering those days. I don't try to make him feel like he isn't significant in my life, but if I tell him I don't remember something, he takes it personally.

After a few months, we moved yet again. Mom never got along with Mark's family, and I felt like she gave him an ultimatum—his family or her. To this day, I believe she brainwashed him.

Mark said he heard of a good job in Tulsa, Oklahoma, and that's where we moved. At times, I felt like my parents thought more of themselves and not about what was best for my sister and me. Being moved around so much before I was even eight years old took a big toll on me. I'm not sure if I was ever genuinely happy; I wasn't even sure what that emotion was. Mark and my mom engaged in a lot of heated, aggressive arguments, and apparently, the apple didn't fall too far from the tree because so did Jane and me.

Life was toxic, and I hadn't lived much of it yet. I was enrolled in a new elementary school in first grade and I hated it almost immediately. There was a tree of hatred growing inside me that I couldn't stop watering. Everything seemed too good to be true, and I needed to protect my heart from being broken. The school sucked the life out of me; everyone there was mean. I didn't fit in because I was the new kid. Not a single kid wanted to be my friend, so at recess, I walked the track alone. The kids must have learned their behavior from the teacher because she was even worse. Her name was Mrs. Muffin Head—that's what I called her because her hair looked like a huge muffin on her head. The end of the school day might have been the best part for other students, but my day always ended with me being distraught and crying about it.

My mom's solution was to put me in a new school the next year. It wasn't worth arguing about, and at that point, I was so accustomed to going to different schools that I just accepted it. I was only in first grade, yet I had already been in at least three schools; now, I would be in my fourth. Mom kept me home until the new school year began. She was supposed to be homeschooling me, but we would sit on the couch and watch her favorite talk shows and movies, with my schoolbooks scattered on the coffee table. I was a step behind everyone in the next year because I never learned anything, but if anyone had asked me who was on the talk show last week, I could have answered that so fast.

---

CHAPTER NINE

friend

/frend/

noun
a person whom one knows and with whom
one has a bond of mutual affection, typi-
cally exclusive of sexual or family relations

Mom waited about a week before she finally took me to
my new school for the first day of class. The entrance
and open hallways were huge. They had an enclosed
garden in the middle of the school's courtyard that
was filled with beautiful flowers. The school was very
nostalgic in all its beauty.

The principle greeted Mom and me with a smile,
"Hello there! Welcome! I'm the principal here,"
Turning to my mom as she took my little hand, she

said "I'll take great care of her and show her to her class."

My mom seemed hesitant to leave at first and kind of lingered around for a bit. This was strange for her because she usually dropped me off and left quickly. She could see that I was happy standing with the principal—it seemed like she was jealous. I can only assume she had a hard time trusting anyone, considering people in her life kept trying to "kidnap" her children. It also could have been the envy of seeing me have such a connection with my principal, a connection with a woman who wasn't her.

My short legs ran over to my mom, and my arms were stretched out to embrace her. Looking up at her, I said, "It's okay, Mom. I'll be all right."

She nodded in agreement and walked out the front door.

The principal walked me to a closed classroom door, and I immediately got jittery. I felt apprehensive and awkward, especially when she decided to introduce me in front of the class. My expression was like a deer in headlights. My teacher put a comforting hand on my shoulder and told me I could pick any seat that was open.

Looking around the classroom, there weren't many choices, but I eyed two desks. One was right in the middle of class among other kids, and the other desk was in the back row, closest to the door.

A girl was sitting next to that empty seat. She seemed very shy and anxious, like I always felt at my new schools. The girl had shoulder length, frizzy brown hair, and she wore a teal-blue crushed-velvet jacket that had two teal stripes going down the arm, with matching pants. I chose that seat because it was the farthest away from everyone else. I didn't realize it then, but that girl would end up being my forever friend.

Marianna was her name. No one wanted to sit by her because they all thought she was weird, and the other kids would snicker about her. Everyone probably assumed I was weird too, but that was okay. At the time, I just wanted to sit down.

Marianna and I didn't talk much that first day. When class was dismissed, she was gone before I even zipped up my backpack. The next day, though, we chatted a bit, and she loaned me a pencil. Within days, we were making jokes and getting in trouble for talking too much.

I remember the first day I went over to her house. Marianna lived exactly two blocks from my house. As we slowed the car to pull into the gravel driveway, my mom asked, "Is this green thing her house?" It *was* an ugly-looking house—a deep green with a small front door on the outside of the garage.

"Yep!" I yelled as I jumped quickly from the car, slammed the door, and ran to the house.

Marianna had three cats, a very old one with long charcoal fur; a short-haired, chunky tabby; and the tabby's son. She lived with just her mom. Her dad wasn't around, and her brother was in and out of the house.

I practically lived at Marianna's house. Jane got jealous because I didn't need her like I used to. Marianna was like the sister I never had. My mom was envious of Marianna's mom and would accuse her of stealing me away. At Marianna's house, however, I was getting the attention that I didn't receive at home, and my mom didn't understand that.

We made up weird games, like VolleyTenniSoc, which was a combination of volleyball, tennis, and soccer. It was a silly game, but we were entertained for hours. I was the biggest klutz ever. Anywhere we went, I somehow would end up getting hurt. Marianna still mentions the time I rode my bike into a concrete ditch in front of her house. I was looking back at her letting her know I was going home to grab more clothes, not paying attention to the sidewalk, and then my face became one with the concrete. I'll never live that down, but if it had been Marianna who did that, I wouldn't let her live it down either.

A boy down the street had a crush on me, but I was

not interested in him; I thought he was dorky and weird. He always came over when he saw us outside playing in Marianna's yard. The neighbor boy put a hula hoop around the cable satellite antenna and called it the Love Circle. He stood in it and tried to convince me that I should join him in the love circle. He lifted the hula hoop above his waist and sang, "Come on, Elle, get in the loooooove circle!"

Marianna and I looked at each other, burst out laughing, and went inside. When he finally got the hint that I didn't like him, he started picking on me. One day, I was outside playing with a metal rod, and he tried to take it from me, so I stood on it.

"You should just leave!" I shouted at him.

"No!" he yelled back at me, then he grabbed the rod from under my foot. When he did, the rod ricocheted up, and when it came back down it sliced open the side of my calf. I screamed bloody murder, and he took off running back to his house. He never spoke to me again.

My mom showed up with her doctor kit ready to do surgery, but she realized the cut was too deep and that I needed to go to the ER. She insisted that I tell her where the boy lived so she could have a "word" with his parents. I lied and told her he was just visiting. She looked right at me seriously and said, "If I ever find out who his parents are, I'll sue them."

Danger should have been my middle name since I consistently looked for dumb and dangerous stuff to do. Marianna was smart and would just watch me being stupid. No wonder we made such a perfect pair of friends. We were two peas in a pod. Marianna was the yin to my yang. She was more balanced and rational; I was impulsive and silly.

One night, I dozed off on the couch. I opened my eyes to my mom hovering over me. While nudging me to wake up she said, "Elle, wake up. It's Marianna on the phone."

I thought I was dreaming because she never liked talking on the phone. With a froggy voice, I answered, "Hello?"

Muffled tears and quiet weeping were all I heard at first. Then Marianna told me that her house had caught on fire, and it was barely standing. I thought I was still dreaming as I got up to go over to her house.

I was absolutely devastated for her. I could see the smoke rising and turning in the air above us. Her family lost practically everything, but I was afraid this would mean she'd have to move away. I spent the following nights with them in a hotel that the fire rescue got for them.

Marianna and I were both ecstatic when her mom

found out they could move into the duplex that was connected to mine, but I also despised it because my mom would be only a wall away from us.

Middle school was starting, and I was excited that Marianna would be joining me there. My heart sank when we got handed our class schedules and saw that we had absolutely no classes together, not even lunch. Still, we sat next to each other on the school bus, ate breakfast together every morning, and walked the halls together before the first bell rang. When we saw each other in the hall, we passed notes that we had written in our classes. Marianna and I folded the notes differently each time, and we "spilled all the tea" about everyone—that means we shared all of our secrets and the latest drama with each other. Marianna always started her letters by telling me she had gone through a whole pack of gum in one day. She got tired of kids always asking her for gum, so she started selling one piece for twenty-five cents. Nothing ever fazed us because we had each other.

Seventh grade was just like sixth grade; we had absolutely no classes together. During sixth grade, Marianna had made a few new friends, and I was afraid Marianna would replace me with someone else. I didn't have anyone else in my life but her. I had a constant fear of being replaced because I was missing so much love in my home life. Despite my fears, our friendship remained strong—strong enough to survive the rest of middle school.

High school was starting soon; the kids I befriended in middle-school had become assholes in high school, so I didn't even consider them acquaintances. I was relieved I still had Marianna. We went to get our schedules together, and again, I was just as disappointed as I was in middle school—we had *no* classes together, and this time, our classes were on opposite sides of the school.

We hardly saw each other, besides walking to school and home together. Regardless of meeting new people throughout high school, we stayed best friends. Marianna and I never skipped class, but sometimes we would pretend we were ill so we could stay home that day and just hang out. Every morning before class began, we would walk the halls together. We always had so many stories to tell one another.

Eighteen years later, I'm pleased to say that our friendship is thriving, and I couldn't imagine it being any other way.

Marianna,

We have never been the emotional type of friends. We're just weird like that, but I want to tell you how much you mean to me. You were always there for me, no matter what. You stayed by my side, even when it would have been so easy for you to leave. You were always there with a listening ear for me to vent to about everything that was going on at home. You never judged me, though. You never made me feel bad for what I was going through or for having a mom like mine.

You've always been a trooper because I can only imagine how hard it must have been. We created fun and happy memories, and they helped fill in all the bad ones I had. You hated half of my boyfriends, but you put up with them for me. You put up with so much, and I am so grateful for that. Thank you for never giving up on me or our friendship. You were one of the best things to ever happen to me. I really do love you a lot.

Elle

CHAPTER TEN

—

ex·pose
/ikˈspōz/

verb
make (something) visible by uncovering it

Freshman year of high school was when I met Aaron. We were in freshman orientation together since our last names were quite close in the alphabet. Homeroom was boring, kind of like a study hall, but the first thing I noticed was how cute he was. He was wearing a white T-shirt with red basketball shorts and matching high-top sneakers. (This was a popular style when I was in high school.) He must have thought I was cute too because he switched seats to be next to my desk.

Another girl, who was sitting next to him before he moved, looked furious that he moved next to me.

We only had orientation for a week, and she shot me eye daggers every day. No matter what I was doing, I could feel her glare burning right through my soul. She would see Aaron pass notes to me and would roll her eyes, but he had such a flirty grin on his face when I would unfold his notes. One of them read "You're beautiful."

The class bell rang, and I took my seat in the next class, smiling ear to ear. Aaron made me feel butterflies instantly and I absolutely adored that feeling. Each morning, I would sit at my desk and find a note. He was so sweet, and I always looked forward to that class, even with the girl who was jealous and had nothing better to do than whisper about Aaron and me to her friends.

Finally, on the last day of that class, he walked up to me as the bell rang and asked me if I would be his girlfriend. Completely smitten by him, I immediately answered yes.

Little did I know that I would come to regret my answer. I didn't realize that he was becoming a bad person because the "love" I had for him was blinding. My vision only allowed me to see that boy on the first day of school who told me I was beautiful. He was the sun, and I had stared at it for too long.

My mom wouldn't let me go to his house because he lived with just his dad and brother. It was so unfair, and I thought the only reason she said no was that she thought women were much better in charge. A little piece of me, however, hoped that maybe she cared about my safety. She didn't know these guys at all, but she never verbalized that was the reason. The rebellious teenager that I was snuck out to Aaron's house, lying by saying I was staying with Marianna. My mom never found out.

In love at fourteen years old, that sounds completely idiotic now that I'm an adult. Aaron could do no wrong in my eyes, but at the time, I wasn't even sure what was *right* in a relationship. He started coming over to my house every so often to hang out. One evening, we were watching TV in the living room when he asked me if I wanted to go down on him.

"No, I don't want to," I said "Plus, my mom is home." Sex wasn't something I had learned about because my mom refused to put me in a sex-ed class, and I never had "the birds and the bees" talk either.

Aaron seemed annoyed and continued to try to convince me to do it. He loved me, and this was what people did when they were in love, right? Wrong. I ended up doing it out of fear that he might break up with me if I didn't. As soon as my mouth made contact with his penis, I instantly pulled my head up. I didn't like it one bit, but he forced me back down with his hands on the back of my head. Again, and again, I tried pulling back up but he kept his hand firmly placed until he finished in my mouth.

I immediately ran into the bathroom because I felt like I was going to vomit. Confused and appalled, I looked at myself in the mirror and began to sob at the girl looking back. The girl I knew was gone; the one looking back wasn't familiar. I couldn't let anyone find out, especially my mom, so I cleaned myself up. I wiped the tears with the back of my hand and slapped on a smile.

After he had me go down on him, I continued to be his girlfriend. I was the epitome of young and dumb. One night, Aaron was visiting while my mom was cleaning up her room. She told us we could watch movies in the living room. He and I were snuggled up together on the couch. When the movie came to an end, I went to the bathroom, while he went to get another drink from the kitchen. I opened the door to come out, and I saw him walking slowly from the kitchen, in a zombie-like way.

It was dark in the house, and I was creeped out,

since the movie we had just finished was a horror movie. I pleaded playfully, "Aaron, stop it! That's not funny."

He started laughing, and my mom came rushing into the room.

"What's going on in here?" she asked.

Still giggling, I said, "We're just playing and joking around."

"Okay," she said, "I have a friend coming over in a little bit. One more movie, and that's it." She seemed annoyed as she walked back to her room.

The living room was dark, and it was just Aaron and me.

He leaned over to me and squeezed my ass. "You look so damn hot in those shorts," he said with a smirk.

My shorts were from Hollister—the very short ones that most young girls wore. My mom said that they were practically underwear. They were cut like Daisy Dukes with distressed holes in them. Blushing, I quickly replied, "Thanks." I jumped up from the couch to switch the movie. I picked up *A Cinderella Story*— my all-time favorite movie that I had seen a thousand times, but what was one more?

"What did you pick?" he asked.

I smiled, "You'll just have to wait and see."

"Come sit on my lap," he said, patting his legs and motioning for me to sit. Aaron looked at me like he was mentally undressing me.

I slowly walked over to him and playfully said no. As I started to sit next to him, he grabbed my hips and pulled me toward him. I didn't think anything of it—until I felt his hands moving my shorts and underwear over.

"Wh-what are you doing?" I asked, but he only shushed me. I immediately froze, and then something started to happen. He pulled me down onto his penis. There were so many emotions running through my mind, but they were overruled by the excruciating pain and the feeling of my insides being ripped apart. I clutched the couch cushions on both sides of me and tried to push myself back up, but he held my hips so tight. Time stood still, everything around me was moving as I tried so damn hard to take my mind to another place. I was at the beach, watching the waves crash into the rocks. The sun was so bright that I had to squint my eyes, but then the sky started swirling, and it got darker. The charcoal-gray clouds enveloped me. The beach I had placed myself on had become black.

Suddenly, I was hit with déjà vu—this feeling was all too familiar to me. Just days before, he had forced my head down on him, and now he was forcing me on his lap. I could feel myself start to bleed from the skin tearing. I tried to speak, but no words came out. I felt disgusting. My heart was pounding so hard that I could feel it deep within my stomach, and tears filled my eyes. I didn't blink so they wouldn't fall. I didn't want him to see me cry. He knew I wanted him to stop. With every, "I don't like this," came the whispered responses of "Shhh, you're okay." He never let go of my hips; he was controlling the motion of my body by moving me up and down on him.

I was his puppet, and the strings to control me were attached to my hips. Time felt like it stopped, and I went somewhere else in my mind again. This time there was no beach, no sun, and no ocean, just complete darkness. Instantly, I wished he'd never come over. I could hear the sound of *A Cinderella Story* playing through the speakers and I wished I was the princess dancing with Austin Ames in the pergola instead of in this hell. My face was extremely hot, and my ears felt like they were melting off. I was screaming at myself in my head asking why I was so stupid and why I had to put on another movie.

A knock at the door snapped me back to reality and ultimately saved me from anything going further. We

both almost jumped out of our skins when we heard it.
I thought, *"Oh, thank God, my mom's friend is here!"* I
used all the strength I could muster up to push myself
off him. I answered the door after I adjusted my underwear and shorts.

Her friend greeted me with a hug, and I motioned in
the direction where my mom was. My eyes wandered
around; I couldn't even look at Aaron as I walked to
the bathroom. I heard him mutter that he now had
blue balls as I walked past him.

I shut the door fast and leaned against the wall. I
sank to the floor, gently crying. The space between my
legs was aching, but I tried to ignore it. I didn't even
want to look at my underwear because I was afraid of
what I might see. I turned on the faucet and ran my
hands under the warm water, splashing it onto my face
make it look like I wasn't crying before walking back
into the living room.

Aaron's dad was supposed to pick him up on his
way home from his evening shift as a jail cell officer,
but I wanted him out of my house right then. I took a
deep breath and turned the knob. Instead of walking
back to the couch, I walked into my mom's bedroom.

"Mom, I'm getting really tired, would you and your
friend care to take Aaron home?"

She seemed shocked and asked if I was sure. I nodded.

Aaron acted like everything was fine as we all walked to the car in the driveway. The two-mile drive to his house went by in a blur. I remember watching out the car window and seeing the trees zooming by like they were just smudges. I don't think I said a word because I was still in disbelief and so furious with myself—but especially with him.

My mom's voice pulled me out of the trance as she announced that we were at his house.

He opened the car door, turned to me expectantly and asked, "You gonna hug me or not?"

Looking forward, I clenched my jaws, said *no* and shut the door. As he walked toward his front porch, my mom turned around in the seat and asked, "Is everything all right?"

I kept my eyes glued to the window because I felt all the emotions build up as the car pulled away from the curb. "We got into a fight," I explained. As we drove back to the house, I watched the birds freely fly in the sunset sky, and I imagined what it would be like to soar and fly so far away from this place.

When we got home, I went straight to bed and didn't speak the rest of the night. I wanted to tell

Marianna, but I was ashamed and felt so stupid for letting this happen. She had never liked him anyway, so I was afraid she would say, "Told you so!" I didn't know I needed someone to be with me throughout this. I should have just told her.

Aaron would pass me in the halls at school, and I avoided him and his text messages like the plague. He would text me things like, "It's normal for people to have sex," and "I'm sorry." The sight of him nauseated me.

For the next couple of months, the first day of my period sent me straight to the emergency room. That first menstrual cycle was so bad. I was at Marianna's house, hunched over the edge of the tub to put pressure on my stomach. I couldn't keep food down, and the doctors said I was bleeding way more than what was normal. It took a second emergency room visit for my mom to find out exactly what had happened. She was beyond livid, and Mark was getting ready to go to his house to have a "word" with him. My mom ended up calling the police.

An extremely tall gentleman approached the porch. I couldn't quite read his name badge under the bright porch light. He had barely stepped inside when my mom started talking with him about everything that had happened.

The officer wasn't there to talk to my mom—I could see the annoyance on his face—but she wouldn't stop talking. She finally figured out she needed to shut up because he threatened to leave before he motioned for me to talk to him in the kitchen. He asked me what happened. I was overwhelmed with emotions, so the waterworks started flowing from my red eyes. I blubbered as I spoke and told him everything. When I finished talking, I finally took a deep breath, and he gave me a blank stare. He sighed as he told me it sounded consensual.

My ears started ringing while he continued to explain how and why it was consensual. My mom heard him; she immediately went into mama-bear mode and started screaming at him. The officer held his hand up to cut my mom off and told her that if I didn't want it, I should have said no—even though I had just told the officer I had told Aaron to stop multiple times. He ignored that.

My world shattered around me. I was so lost. Was I wrong? Was it consensual? Maybe I did want it. Maybe my shorts were giving him a signal, and I didn't truly say no. After the officer left, I told my mom that maybe he was right; maybe I did want it. I honestly wasn't sure. It didn't occur to me at the time that I didn't have to be held down for it to be considered raped or sexual assault. I didn't want it, but the officer convinced me that I not only had wanted it but had asked for it. Aaron did it out of love, right? Being told I *did* want to have sex with him made me question everything. I even felt bad for how I had treated him afterward. Leave it to a man to bully me into accepting that it was my fault.

It didn't take Aaron long to start flirting with other girls, and some fucked-up part of me was jealous. Of course, the main person he flirted with was the same girl who had been mean to me in orientation. He was going to toss me away like a piece of trash after everything we had been through—after he had sex with me.

A while back when we were dating, I found out he had a second cell phone that he told me he randomly had "found." He told me he wanted to switch his number to it, but that was a huge lie, considering when I walked through the front doors of the school the next day, all the jocks were staring and snickering at me.

I met up with Marianna and asked, "Do you have any idea what's going on?" She looked as confused as I did, and shook her head then shrugged her shoulders. When I sat down at my desk in first period, a student office worker came in and handed my teacher a pass. The teacher said that I needed to go to the principal's office.

Walking through the empty halls, I wasn't sure what I was walking into. I opened the door to the office—and saw Aaron in the waiting area with a smug look on his face.

The look on his face disgusted me, so I kept my eyes glued to the floor as I walked into the principal's office. The principal held up the phone that Aaron had told me he found. The principal then asked me if I knew whose phone it was.

"That's Aaron's. He told me a while ago that it was his," I said with confusion.

He shook his head and let out a deep sigh. Dead silence filled the room. My palms were getting sweaty, and I was anxious. What was the big deal? The principal looked at me and explained that it never belonged to Aaron. It was the football captain's phone. He had reported it stolen when he opened his locker and saw that it was gone. When the principal had told me he stole the phone, I remembered when he had stolen a bracelet from one of the football players lockers; the same locker the phone came from.

That asshole I thought. *He lied to me yet again.* Nothing could have prepared me for what came out of the principal's mouth next.

He asked me if I knew what was on the cell phone.

My heart began to beat faster as I realized that I had sent Aaron some nude photos, but I hadn't sent them to *that* phone—or at least I thought I hadn't. The principal had a very sympathetic look on his face when he told me that there were at least fifteen pictures of me, fully nude or changing. He said that many of them appeared to have been taken without knowledge.

My jaw dropped at the thought of the pictures I had taken for only Aaron's eyes to see. There were pictures of me in my bra and even completely nude photos of my boobs and vagina. I was stunned but I managed to stammer "Ca-ca-can I see them?"

"They have been deleted," the principal said.

I was somewhat relieved because that meant no one else would see them. Right? Wrong. The kid from who Aaron had stolen the phone had shown the entire football team the night before at the game. I couldn't believe it! At some of my most vulnerable moments, Aaron had dared to take pictures of me without telling me. I knew he took some of them, but he always swore he'd delete them. I was so humiliated. I just wanted to dig a hole, crawl into it, and die.

Aaron was telling everyone we had sex, and the icing on the cake was that so many students had seen all the parts of me that were supposed to be hidden.

Rumors were going around that I was a slut, but mainly, I figured that was because my sister Jane had gotten around. If people thought I was a slut before, though, then this wasn't helping my case at all.

The worst part of it was that it really was my fault. It was my fault for ever trusting Aaron and believing every single word he said to me. Aaron told me he loved me, and my knees buckled. I opened myself up to him, and he let everyone else in. That day, I finished eating lunch and doing homework in the office, but I knew that word of this had already gotten around. I bottled all these moments and didn't talk about them with anyone.

Marianna knew, but she never told me. My mom was called by the principal and was informed of what happened. The next day I was sent to the office again. When I walked in, I saw my mom sitting at a long conference table with the principal and some teachers. "I'm taking Elle out of school since Aaron isn't getting expelled," she said. My heart broke, because I was being punished but Aaron never got into any trouble.

The incident got brushed under the rug, but I suffered internally for it. Eventually, it all became old news. I definitely had the worst freshman year experience on record.

---

CHAPTER ELEVEN

clue·less
/ˈklo͞oləs/

adjective
having no knowledge, understanding, or
ability

After the fiasco of a relationship with Aaron, I started
to change. When I returned to school for my soph-
omore year, I barely had friends because Aaron's
friends had taken his side, and I had become such a
"whore" in everyone's eyes. Girls threatened to fight
me if they caught their boyfriends looking in my direction. The guys would try to sleep with me because
they all thought I was easy, but when I told them I
wouldn't, it just caused more problems and more rumors. Some guys started a rumor that I was giving

hand jobs behind the stairwell. I desensitized myself to all the bullshit that was happening around me. At least I still had Marianna on my team.

Marianna and I never had deep conversations about feelings and whatnot. I wasn't sure if she'd ever heard the rumors about me or if she just didn't give a shit because I was her best friend, and she knew the actual truth. I want to think it was the latter.

"You don't want to get mixed up with a girl like me. I'm a loner, a rebel." -Peewee Herman

I was a loner, and I became a rebel. My mom controlled my life so that contributed to my having close to zero friends.

At sixteen years old, I didn't have a car and didn't know the first thing about driving, so I told a lot of lies to my parents about what I was doing. For example, I would say I was going one place with one person, but instead, I would go somewhere else with a completely different person. No matter who I ended up meeting or where I went, Marianna was always with me. There were times when I felt so bad for lying to Marianna's mom because she was such a good person, but we were young, dumb, and wanted to have fun.

We would devise a plan, and I would tell my mom I was staying at Marianna's house for the weekend.

Then we would tell Marianna's mom that we were going to my house. Neither of them checked with the other because we had grown up together. They trusted us, and that worked on our behalf. Neither of us had cars so we told her mom we were walking to my house, but we'd be picked up by a couple of our friends at the fast-food place on the corner. We would end up going to bonfires or public parks and drink our livers away.

One night, we stopped by a gas station, and I started talking to a guy outside. We chatted about what Marianna and I were doing and our plans for the night. He said he was waiting for his friends to get him, but they hadn't shown up yet, and he was ready to leave. I found out he was twenty-one, and I saw that as a golden opportunity that I jumped at.

"You can hang out with us, and our friends can give you a ride if you get us some booze," I said, batting my eyelashes at him. I felt that since I was being called a slut, I might as well be one.

"All right," he said, "You talked me into it." His house became the official party house for us, and I threw a party there practically every weekend. (This gave a whole new meaning to *dumb*. I was extremely naive when it came to having a good time. I should have thought twice before doing something like that.)

News of the parties I threw spread like wildfire throughout the school, and soon, even the "top dogs" at school came to the parties. I was becoming one of the cool, popular kids. As soon as I walked through the school doors, students I didn't even know waved hello. I took advantage of this because the rumors about me had stopped. Every weekend, Friday and Saturday and even some Sunday nights, I was at the party house.

Alcohol had become a new lifestyle for me. School and my classes were no longer important in my mind; it was only my new friends from school and my other best friend, Green Apple Smirnoff. Marianna only came to the parties sometimes.

My 4.0 GPA tanked pretty fast because my new-found popularity and the feeling I got from other people and alcohol was a greater chase for me. I dropped out of high school and went to college, I continued to drink and party.

When I turned eighteen years old, Marianna and I started going to the local gay bar. Sometimes our friend would come with us, and we would look for someone at the bar who was twenty-one or older to buy us a bottle of green apple vodka down the road at the liquor store. After getting the cheap bottle of vodka, we would slam it back behind a dumpster in the alley. I always managed to find alcohol. I was the lion, and alcohol was the gazelle.

Drinking and going out to the bar had become a regular thing, like brushing my teeth. I lived up to the song by Kesha. The rush I would feel from not remembering the night before was exhilarating when I woke up the next day. It was like I was pressing the backspace button on the keyboard to delete it, and the next day would be my clean slate. I didn't think I was addicted to alcohol; it just came with the party lifestyle. I loved the fast-paced party life.

Mark had moved into his own place, so it was just my mom, Jane, and me living together. The fighting between us got worse, and my mom constantly reminded me of what an awful child I was. That just added to me wanting to drink and party harder. I wanted to keep myself busy, but I was doing it the wrong way. I barely remember anything of importance from the time I was seventeen to twenty years old. Most people think they know who they are at that age, but they don't. Vodka and I tried to erase all the hurt I had felt, but no matter how much I consumed, my emotions didn't go away. The emotions lived in the back of my mind, rent-free; they collected in their own personal recycle bin that was never emptied. Nevertheless, I trekked on and kept stuffing those emotions away.

I met a guy at the bar that allowed minors in. Marianna and I would go every weekend, and he soon became my boyfriend. He played on a local APFL football team and acted like a hotshot. He usually had his best friend with him, who was smitten with Marianna. The two of us started staying at their house all the time, and, of course, we'd drink. At the time I was nineteen years old, and Marianna had just moved into a new apartment with her mom.

Anytime we didn't stay at the boy's house, I stayed at her apartment; I had practically moved in. Marianna's nieces and nephews were over for the weekend since the school was out for the summer. It was such a humid, hot day that just walking outside to my car and back inside caused me to sweat through my shirt profusely. We decided to go to the pool. Everyone at the apartment complex had that same idea.

Marianna and I were tanning as the kids played with some other kids in the water. A guy and his girlfriend were sitting in chairs about five feet from us, and a super-cute toddler came running over to us. The little boy stopped in his tracks and just grinned at me.

"Hi," I said with a smile.

"Hey! Leave those girls alone. Come back here," his mom yelled to him. The little boy laughed as he turned to run back to his mom.

"It's okay," I said to the little boy's dad. "Your little boy is so cute."

Marianna's and my friendship with the boy's dad blossomed that day. We all stayed at the pool for quite a while, just talking. He told us his name was Andy. We all got to know each other by asking simple questions, and we found out he was only a couple of years older than us. He and his child's mom were co-parenting the little boy.

Andy came over all the time to Marianna's apartment, and he got to meet my boyfriend. They hit it off instantly and became friends too. The four of us would go to the club together constantly, and I loved that I had a good guy friend that my boyfriend wasn't bothered by or super-sensitive about.

My boyfriend had an away game in St. Louis, and I couldn't go because I had to work. He promised me that time would go fast and that he'd be home before I knew it. I was working at a snack shop inside a big retail store when I received a text from him: "I have to tell you something."

My insides instantly twisted together. At that

moment, I was standing by the popcorn and hot dog machines. *Pop, pop, pop* came from the popcorn machine as I stood there, frozen.

I replied: "What is it?" My body tensed, and tears started to fall as I read the words on the screen:

"I'm sorry. I hooked up with my ex."

Heartbroken and shaken, I couldn't muster up the courage or the strength to reply. He never sent any texts after that; even without my reply. That showed me that he didn't give two shits about me.

Mark dropped me off at Marianna's so I could tell her the news. I was sobbing on her shoulder when she came up with the brilliant idea of going out that night to take my mind off my break-up. Marianna texted Andy to let him know what happened, and he came over as soon as he could. He was extremely comforting and made me feel less lousy. Andy comforted me by telling me that my now ex-boyfriend wasn't worth my tears.

In the past week, we had celebrated Andy's twenty-first birthday at the club, so he came up with the idea of getting us a bottle of liquor. His aunt planned on taking us downtown to a club Andy loved. Marianna and I didn't hesitate to agree. We waited on the park bench in the courtyard of the apartments while he went to the liquor store. He came back with our favorite, Southern Comfort Original. The three of us passed the bottle around, joking and laughing as we always did. I was already feeling a lot better.

They gave me the last bit that was left at the bottom of the bottle. "Thank you, guys," I said as I gulped down the last shot. Once I finished with what was left in the bottle, we sat in silence. With everything so still and quiet, my thoughts all rushed in, and I started to get sad again. Andy and Marianna weren't going to let that happen.

He called his aunt to come to get us and told Marianna and me to get ready for the club. We walked back to her apartment to get dressed. I put on some music to get us hyped as we curled our hair and put on our makeup. Singing and laughing with Marianna made me even more excited to go out. I paired my over-the-shoulder Marilyn Monroe top with a black pencil skirt and neon-yellow high-heeled pumps. When we were ready, I texted Andy, and soon we were pulling up in front of the bar. I stumbled out of the back seat, so Andy quickly grabbed my side to steady me.

We all laughed as we walked to the door to pay. The bar had a dress code in which all females had to wear heels to be allowed in. Marianna and I were in the clear, but when Andy got to the door, the security guards turned him away because he didn't have a belt on and his shorts were too saggy. He was pissed. Marianna and I were annoyed, but we were drunk, so we just laughed.

Andy's aunt picked us up again and took us to his mom's so he could get a belt. I kept fading in and out of consciousness. I wasn't even sure where we were at that point. It was like I was on a Tilt-A-Whirl ride, and everything was spinning around me. Cars and streetlights flew by my window. Startled awake, I heard someone say, "We're here," as we pulled up to a different club.

We all hopped out of the car; it was a blur for me as we walked in. Andy told us to find a table, and he would get us some drinks. We nodded as he walked to the bar. He joined us shortly afterward. I downed the drink he brought and then begged Marianna to dance with me. I had to pull her onto the dance floor. The music was loud, and all I could feel was the beat inside of my head; that's all that mattered.

Suddenly, I remembered I needed to change my tampon, so I grabbed Marianna's hand and turned to Andy. "We're going to go to the bathroom." Somehow, I managed to do my business, but later, I wouldn't remember that Marianna and I took a picture in the full-length mirror until I looked through my pictures. When we got back to the table, I went back to the dance floor, alone this time. There was yelling and name-calling between me and some other girls, and I then I felt Andy's hands pulling me away as I swung at one of them, barely missing the girl's face. We were thrown out by the bouncer before anything else could happen. Andy called his aunt to come back and get us.

I fell asleep on the way back to the apartments. I was extremely plastered so Marianna had to help me walk to his aunt's apartment. Marianna only lived one building over from his aunt's, but we couldn't go back to Marianna's apartment when we were drunk. We planned on sobering up and then sneaking back to her place.

His aunt asked with concern if I was okay.

"Of course!" I replied, "Where is your bathroom, and do you have any tampons?"

She chuckled and then showed me where the bathroom and tampons were. I told her I was hungry, so she put some chicken nuggets in the oven for me before she left with her guy friend to go back out; it was only midnight.

When I came out of the bathroom, Marianna was

sitting in the big recliner, and Andy was on the couch so I plopped down next to him. I sobered up a bit as we watched TV; I was getting tired. Andy put an arm around me and asked if I was thirsty. I nodded, so he got up to get me a drink. Then Marianna and I heard him laugh from the kitchen.

We both asked, "What are you laughing at?"

While cackling, he informed us that my nuggets were burned.

We had forgotten they were in the oven. He returned to the couch with the one slightly burned piece of chicken and then handed me a drink. He laughed and said, "That one was the least burned of them all."

I thought he was bringing me water, but instead, he brought me an opened Smirnoff Ice. I was so dehydrated from all the alcohol and the burned chicken sticking in my throat that I chugged the Smirnoff.

Darkness. My mind went blank. *Where am I? Am I dreaming?* No, I wasn't dreaming. I slowly opened my eyes only to see darkness once again. My vision couldn't focus. It was like a person waking up without their glasses. *Heavy breathing. Where is that coming from?* Confusion set in because it wasn't my breathing. Hands were moving on my body, and I started blinking as I squinted around the room.

Looking down, I saw that Andy was underneath me. He was inside of me. My voice caught in my throat, and my limbs felt like they weren't connected to my body. I was essentially paralyzed. I could feel my lips forming the word *stop*—and finally, it escaped my mouth.

"*Stop!*" I shouted at him as I frantically looked for Marianna, but she wasn't there.

Within seconds, I was flailing my arms and still screaming for him to stop. I was fighting to get off him, but he grabbed my hips so tight and kept pushing inside me. He kept telling me I wanted it and that I had asked for it. I felt déja vu yet again. My eyes filled with moisture, but the tears didn't fall. I was numb—body, mind, and soul. I know he saw the terror in my eyes as he moaned. I was still fighting for him to let go of me.

I screamed but only a whisper escaped my lips. "No, I never wanted this." Finally, I managed to pull myself from his grip and fell onto the floor. I quickly stood up on my wobbly legs. He lay there on the futon with a grimace on his face. His pants were still undone, like he was expecting me to get back on him and continue. I spat the words, "How could you!"

He gave me a crooked smile and said again that I had asked for it.

I never asked for it, and I never wanted it. I reached my hand in between my legs and felt the blood running down. It sent me into an immediate panic. I was still wearing my clothes. My shirt was still tucked into my skirt like it was when we were at the club, but my skirt was rolled up over my waist. I wasn't even sure where I was as I searched for my underwear.

I couldn't find them, and I never did. I spotted my tampon near the futon on the floor—the tampon he had taken out of me. I didn't want to be near him. I couldn't even fathom looking at him. I ran out the bedroom door and saw that the TV was still on. Marianna was asleep on the recliner, and as I reached down to pick up my heels, I yelled for her to wake up. Desperately, I continued yelling at her to leave with me as I pulled the front door open.

Marianna looked so confused. "What's going on?"

While looking at her through my mascara stained and blood-shot eyes, a tears rolled down my cheek. "We have to get out of here. I'll tell you everything once we're away from him."

Marianna jumped out of the chair as Andy came out of the room, telling me to wait up. I was hysterical and couldn't even look at him. We made it down one flight of stairs when my legs gave out beneath me. I started crying as I sat on the landing.

Marianna was so frightened and didn't know what was going on; she insisted we get out of the building before Andy came out. I was stumbling through the courtyard and kept falling. Marianna tried her best to help me walk. I staggered into the side of the building and started vomiting. I couldn't stop. Green bile was the only thing that came out. I tried to wipe my mouth between my whimpering, but it didn't help.

She pulled me up and told me that we could go to the laundry room. Andy wouldn't know the code to get in because he didn't live there. We couldn't go back to Marianna's yet since it was 3:00 a.m., and her mom thought we were staying at my house. We stayed in the laundry room until 7:00 a.m., and I told Marianna everything.

"He brought me that open Smirnoff, and now I can't remember how or when I fell asleep. I was terrified when I woke up, and I also thought you just left me there," I explained.

"I never would have left you," she said. "I remember when he picked you up, I asked where he was taking you. It worried me, but he told me that you didn't look comfortable sleeping sitting up. My eyelids were heavy then, but I stayed awake to make sure he came back out but then I fell asleep when he returned."

Andy had it all planned. He had roofied my Smirnoff and then waited for Marianna to fall asleep so he could come in the room to rape me. How long did he have this planned? Marianna gave me a pair of her underwear when we went back to her apartment then I cried myself to sleep and slept for the rest of day, only getting up to use the restroom. I didn't eat because if I had, it would have come back up. I was so disgusted with myself and Andy. I didn't want to talk to anyone. Marianna and I made a pact that we would never tell a single soul what had happened. I regret that I decided to make that pact. It would be a mistake that I so wish that I could take back.

I blamed myself. It was my fault for putting myself in that situation. I didn't go to the police. I didn't even tell my parents or see a doctor. My thoughts were that if I told anyone, they would frown upon me, or they wouldn't believe me, like with the Aaron situation.

Months slipped by, but it never got easier to forget.

Occasionally, I would still cry myself to sleep, and I would lie when someone would ask how I was doing. Slapping on a fake smile, I would look at them and simply say, "I'm fine."

I had to bury that nightmare of a night deep inside me. I didn't see Andy around much after that night, but if I did, I made sure to hide or run in the other direction. I was crushed—mentally, emotionally, and physically—but he walked around like it was nothing. The pain I was feeling was excruciating, but Andy waltzed around like a normal person.

Henry and I started casually dating. He lived in the same apartment complex as Marianna, one floor above, and he told me he was having a small party one night. It started with just us and a few of his friends, but within hours, the apartment was packed with people. All of us were having so much fun playing beer pong, and we made a bet that the losing team had to go streaking around the apartment courtyard. Of course, my partner and I lost, so we were the dumb, naked, drunk people running through the apartments. I loved to be daring and have fun. Henry's friend offered me a pipe; I accepted it and took a couple of puffs of the weed to impress him, I thought. I hadn't smoked but a few times, so I didn't know what was going to happen when it mixed with alcohol. The taste of weed was gross to me, so I stuck to beer for the rest of the night.

After a few beers, I was starting to feel the effects of the weed. My head was spinning but not the tipsy sort of spin I'd experienced with alcohol. I felt like I was on a merry-go-round, being pushed harder and harder, round and round. Lots of spinning, and it seemed to get faster. My head suddenly wasn't connected to my body, or so it seemed. I couldn't keep anything down and ended up on the bathroom floor, over the toilet.

It was super-nice that everyone at the party kept coming to check on me. When people came to the bathroom, all I could see was their heads, floating. Their lips were moving, and their heads were moving but there weren't bodies attached beneath it. I felt like I was dying. My heart was pounding out of my chest, and I couldn't catch my breath. Thinking of it now, I think I gave myself a panic attack, but I had never been as scared in my life as I was at that moment.

I passed out for about thirty minutes because when I came to, the bathroom wasn't spinning anymore. I felt like a complete person again, and everyone's heads got reconnected to their bodies. I went back to the couch and joined Henry and his friends. I looked at a guy who just walked through the door—my heart dropped into my stomach when I realized it was Andy.

All the color and blood in my body washed away, as if I didn't have a pulse. It had been months since he'd raped me, but it felt like I was suddenly taken back to hearing his moans and feeling him holding onto me so tight. That's when the panic took over. I grabbed Henry's hand and frantically whispered, "That's him! He did it."

Andy knew what he'd done, and it felt like he was proud of it. He looked right at me and then walked to the dining room table, sat down and opened a beer. My hand gripped Henry's hand tighter, and I felt tears flooding my eyes. I couldn't let him see me upset. I didn't want him to think he had won. Andy had only been there for a few minutes when Harry stood up and told him he needed to leave. Andy didn't like that, and I could feel his glare slicing through me. I couldn't look at him. I wasn't one to be afraid of anyone, but I was terrified of him.

Andy made a scene as he got up, and everyone at the party stopped what they were doing to watch. I could feel my head start to spin again. Andy looked at me with his maniac eyes and said, "Fuck you, bitch!" as he stormed through the door to the hallway. When he left, I realized I had been holding my breath. I exhaled and closed my eyes; then I turned to Henry and whispered, "I have to leave. I'm sorry." I stumbled from the couch to the door.

I needed my best friend. I needed Marianna. I

needed to feel safe. My legs carried me down the stairs to her apartment. It was 2:00 a.m., and as I knocked on her door, I threw up in the hallway. I was practically dry heaving because nothing but stomach acid was coming up. My face was soaked with my tears, and as Marianna opened the door, I fell into her arms. Her mom, who, surprisingly, was still awake, ran to the door and began to freak out. She wasn't sure what was wrong, but she was so concerned.

I was a blubbering mess as I tried to choke out the words, but I didn't realize I was yelling that he raped me. No one, other than Marianna, knew that he had done that.

There was a look of horror on her mom's face as her fear escalated. "Who did this to you?" she asked. Everything else she was saying ran together.

That was all I could hear. My ears were burning, and my eyes were on fire. All I could muster was, "He did."

Her mom immediately dialed 911 and then called my parents. Mark and my mom got to the apartment before the cops. It didn't dawn on me what I had done until the cops arrived and asked for all the details. I had to explain that I was at a party where I saw him, and the memories of that night had rushed back. It took so much to keep Mark from going to find Andy. Throughout the next month, I was at the police station practically every week. There was nothing they could do unless I could get a confession out of him. There were times Andy would be on Harry's balcony, and when he saw me in the parking lot, he would try to talk to me as if we were still friends.

It was too late to do a date-rape test, and it was too late for me to be okay.

To this day, I still have times when I beat myself up for not doing anything that night. I didn't ask for help when I needed it the most because I feared the unknown outcome.

I saw Andy downtown on a Friday night, years after that happened, and I still froze up. He had a smirk on his face as he looked my way.

Then I saw him at the club. I was doing a line dance with Marianna when I turned and saw him. I frantically tapped her shoulder, asking, "Is that Andy?"

She didn't see him and assured me that it wasn't; the guy standing there just looked like Andy. It had been eight years since she had seen him, so she didn't know what he looked like anymore. When Andy saw that I got Marianna's attention, he stepped behind his friend that looked similar so he wouldn't be seen.

As we continued dancing, Andy came up behind me and grabbed my hips. I was taken back to that night all over again. When Marianna turned and saw him, she grabbed my hand and pulled me away. He disappeared after giving me an "I won" look. My other friends that were at the club searched for him but had no luck finding him.

I also saw him a couple of times after that, by sheer coincidence but I'm not afraid of him anymore.

Andy,

I don't hate you, but I don't like you. I never will. You took so much from me, and I questioned all of me because of what you did. You broke me. I lost who I was for years because of that night. I thought I deserved it, but I didn't. You just thought you deserved to take whatever you wanted. I have so much pity for you. You have to live with knowing what you did to me and all the other girls for the rest of your life. You didn't win, and I'm way stronger than you'll ever wish to be now. I'll be just fine, but you have to be the one to live with what you did to me in the back of your mind.

Sincerely,
A survivor

If you're going through something like this, know you're not alone. Don't put yourself in a corner like I did. Living with the memory and knowing that my fear was the only thing standing in the way is the worst feeling to have.

If you need help, please ask for it. When you reach your hand up, there will always be someone reaching down to help you.

Healthyplace.com
800.656.HOPE (4673)
#METOO

---

CHAPTER TWELVE

be·lieve

/bəˈlēv/

verb
accept (something) as true; feel sure of the
truth of

I had been picked to work a liquor tasting at a golf tournament with another girl—I'd worked with her previously at the liquor store. It was in another town about forty minutes away, and I drove us in my car. Everyone was so nice and helped us set up our tent on the course. We had been there for a couple of hours, and our boss gave us the okay to drink a little while working. Golfers brought us candy bars and water; in return, we gave them extra shots of the alcohol we had. It was around lunchtime when the maintenance men came to our tent and asked us if we wanted to share a pizza with them.

Pizza sounded good at the moment. I ate about four pieces and drank two bottles of water because I was starving and so thirsty. I only had a few drinks of alcohol by then. The boss of the maintenance men had a son who was about three, and he took a liking to me. I was completely smitten by this little boy and had him sit on my lap on the golf cart. We took selfies on Snapchat together. His favorite filter was the one that gives you a dog nose and ears.

Everyone finished eating, and the workers left the little boy with us as they went to work but said they would be back soon. Only fifteen minutes passed when they returned. They told us about an awesome-tasting Monkey shot they had gotten from another table of shot girls, a few holes over from where we were. They invited me to go with them to bring back a shot for each of us. I barely had a buzz, so I didn't think it would hurt to get another shot, and I had no reason not to trust them.

When I looked at my coworker to get a "go-ahead", she nodded and winked. "That's fine," she said, "Just hurry back with our shots."

The golf cart had a flatbed trailer on the back, and

the youngest guy jumped back there and grabbed my hand to pull me up. They insisted that we wouldn't be gone long, and I believed them. It was as if they knew I was unsure, but they convinced me I could trust them. We stopped to drop the child off with someone, and that was the last time I saw him. As we reached the table with the shot girls, I started to stand up, but the boss insisted, "You stay there. We'll bring one to ya."

Laughing, I replied, "Okay."

When they returned with my shot, I laughed and jokingly said, "You didn't roofie me, right?" Ever since that day, I've always joked about it, but it's a joke that is hiding so much worrying truth.

They laughed too and said they would never do that then they playfully punched my arm. We toasted with the little plastic cups and tilted our heads back. It was extremely hot outside, and the cold purple liquid felt so good sliding down my throat.

I looked around with questioning eyes and asked, "Where's my coworker's shot?"

One of them said "Get back in the cart, and we'll grab her shot on the way back to your tent." At that point, I started to get a little nervous. I was supposed to be working, and they'd told me we were only going to get a Monkey shot. We all got on the golf cart. I was hesitant, but if I had gotten off, I wasn't sure how to get back to where I'd been. I swallowed back my nervousness as the golf cart lurched forward through the bright green grass.

They were all talking and laughing as the youngest worker put his hand on my knee. He whispered to me, "It'll be okay. We'll take you back to her soon." He started moving his hand farther up my leg. It felt like I had cotton in my mouth and couldn't use my words. I immediately smacked his hand and shook my head. I playfully giggled because I didn't want him getting pissed at me and leaving me stranded.

Suddenly, I was hit with a dizzy spell. I was very confused by it because I wasn't that buzzed, and I'd had four slices of pizza in my system. *Why was I feeling this way?* I could feel the wheels on the trailer rolling. I felt like Alice in Wonderland, falling down the rabbit hole. We reached another table. As the golf cart came to a stop, I stumbled to get off the trailer. This time, they helped me down and didn't tell me to wait in the cart.

My body didn't feel like I had any control over it, and I could barely keep my eyes open. The shot girls at that table had Fire ball shots, which I dislike, but I reached out for one because I didn't want them to touch it. We toasted with our little plastic cups again, and I washed my cotton mouth away with the fiery liquid. They laughed and said, "One more!"

I just wanted to go back to my coworker, but I reached for my second shot. When I reached my hand out, the shot girl looked a little concerned about me. "Is she okay?" she asked. "She's fine! She has just had a little too much to drink," one of the guys said while laughing. Once again, we toasted, but as they tilted their heads back, I tossed out the liquid into the sandpit behind me. The shot girl saw me pour out my shot but before I could say anything to her, we were moving again. I could feel myself riding through the golf course, but I couldn't focus my eyes on anything. The last thing I remember was the trees zooming by me in a blur and feeling the tires of the golf cart rolling over rocks.

I woke up face-down near my coworker and the tent. There was so much time I had lost, four hours to be exact. I truly had no recollection of anything since the fire ball shot. Golfers were standing around me with her. I could hear someone on the phone just a few feet away. There were a lot of voices in hushed tones. All of them were talking about me, and I overheard someone say, "We found her unconscious in the grass, just lying here."

My head was pounding from the headache I had, and I felt like I was still asleep as two arms pulled me up into a lawn chair. I reached for my face, but it was numb. My hands reached up to touch my eyes; they were wet with tears and mascara. My face was puffy from crying, but I wasn't even sure why I was crying. I was that sorority girl who just had a rough night out. At least, I looked that way. Tears started to fall as I reached out for some water. I kept trying to tell them I was okay, but the way my face appeared told them differently. I had to wash down the barf I could feel in the pit of my stomach that was trying to come up.

My mind was back in a dark place, and everyone felt so far from me, yet they were all right by my side. I heard a woman telling everyone that the officer was on his way, but it sounded like she was whispering. I couldn't quite gather her words.

The officer pulled up and had me come to his vehicle to speak with him. I told him everything that I could remember. I explained that we had eaten pizza, and I had sobered up. I said there was a little boy with us, and then I didn't see him again. The officer told me there was never a little boy with the maintenance men. I swear to this day that the officer was wrong because I had photos that I had taken with the little boy. I went on to tell him how the youngest guy had touched my leg and tried moving it farther up, but I smacked his hand away.

I pleaded with the officer to find those men. He assured me that he had already spoken with the boss, and he told the officer I had just drunk too much so they dropped me back off at the tent.

That was complete and utter bullshit! It was all a lie! I never stepped foot back under that shady tent, and my coworker told him they never brought me back there. I didn't understand why he wouldn't listen to me. He didn't believe me. Once again, a man in uniform that you're supposed to trust had bullied me into being quiet and pinned it all on me.

I waited thirty minutes for my friend to come to get me to take me home. I was a blubbering emotional mess. "I thought something really bad had happened to you," she said as she cried with me. Something bad did happen. It felt like part of her didn't believe what I said happened.

I'll never know what fully happened that day, and even worse, I'll never know if those men took advantage of me. The memories of those four hours were gone and lost. Once again, an officer that could have helped me seemed to think I was another drunk pretty girl that was out to get someone.

At the end of that day, I was glad I had a friend who could be with me: my cat. When I got home I crawled into my bed, turned on *Moana*, and I cried into my pillow until I fell asleep. Another night when I cried myself to sleep. I never want anyone, even me, to cry herself to sleep again.

fear

/ˈfir/

noun

an unpleasant emotion caused by the belief that someone or something is dangerous, likely to cause pain, or a threat

The things that freak out other people have little to no effect on me. If there's a spider, I'm the one to get it, and it's the same with snakes. If it isn't attacking me, then I won't hurt it. What I fear is people, death, windows, and being alone. These are things that half of humanity isn't that afraid of; at least, not to my knowledge. People scare me because I don't know who's genuine and who's not. We spend our lives making relationships with other people, based on what they tell us.

I have some serious trust issues due to my mom and other people burning that bridge a while back. You might not believe it, but I'm really good at meeting new people and being in the spotlight. But when I'm alone, I turn into an ostrich that hides its head in the sand.

I'm pretty closed off from other people, yet I am afraid of being alone. When something is good, I can't make my mind believe it, so my solution is to ignore it. I run away from the good in my life; my feet are so exhausted from running. I'm unsure of truly knowing who I am. I find it funny that I distance myself from others yet I hate being alone. I've felt so alone in the past that I know now I never want to feel that way. It's a cycle that has never ended—a constant battle of my wanting to be surrounded by others, but instead, I push them away. It's a lose-lose situation for me. I realized that when it rains, it pours.

I've had a recurring nightmare that I was being chased down a never-ending sidewalk at night by a man with no face. I always believed it was my biological dad, yet I just ran and ran. I've also dreamed that I was in a house with stairs everywhere. As I would go up a set of stairs, thinking it would lead me out, I would run into another set of stairs, leading me farther inside. The stairs had me trapped inside this house, and I've always felt trapped and lost in my own life. It's like me dreams want to keep me afraid and sad while I'm asleep.

I am afraid of windows because I have a memory of sleeping in my crib next to a window. My mom and Mark were in the kitchen. The only light in the room came from the hallway and moonlight. I don't recall if I was quite asleep but I heard the screen being removed from the window. Luckily, I had excellent hearing, and I bolted up. I looked behind me and saw that Jane was fast asleep in our mom's bed. Then I heard the quiet sound of the window being pushed up. I quickly jumped from my crib and ran to the kitchen yelling, "Mom! Mom! Someone is trying to come through the bedroom window and get me!"

Mark and my mom jumped up from their seats. My mom grabbed a knife before they ran to the bedroom. Just as the man was reaching his hands in, my mom slammed the window down on his fingers. I heard him back away in pain.

Years later, I was told that the man who tried to come in the room was the older, wealthy man from down the street that my mom was sneaking around to see.

I'm afraid of death, yet I used to slit my wrists and watch the blood seep out. How ironic. I didn't do it because I wanted to die. I did it because I wanted to feel something. I needed to feel something real. I never felt like I was in control of myself, so I did it to be in control. For once, I could pull my own strings, like the puppet others treated me as. I felt like I was just floating above myself. It was like watching a movie being made. I cut myself to bring myself back down to earth and to bring myself back to life.

People cope in different ways, some worse than others, but it's not okay to hurt yourself. It took me a very long time to believe that. I was so hurt by others that I thought, *If they can do it, why can't I?* but I'm stronger now. I finally began to believe that I didn't deserve the hurt or the pain I was holding deep within myself. I chose to stop running. Tomorrow isn't guaranteed, so I soak up as much of today as I can. I don't want to die anymore.

Writing is now my outlet. I can express myself without feeling judged. Even when I'm feeling most alone, I know I will always have my mind and a pen to write with. Try to look on the bright side, even when all you can see are clouds.

I finally learned to love myself.

<u>National Suicide Prevention Lifeline</u>
Call 1-800-273-8255

Available twenty-four hours every day.

Many people have struggles. Unfortunately, some of those people don't have the love and support they need, but I want to try to help as many people that I can. I'll be there for you. If you just need to vent to someone, that can be me. My ears will be open, and I will be ready to listen. My hand will be there for you to grab whenever you are ready.

Please send me a message on Instagram whenever you need to: elle.shane1992